GW01275885

Tausret

Tausret

Forgotten Queen and Pharaoh of Egypt

Edited by

RICHARD H. WILKINSON

OXFORD

UNIVERSITY PRESS

OXFORD
UNIVERSITY PRESS

Oxford University Press, Inc., publishes works that further
Oxford University's objective of excellence
in research, scholarship, and education.

Oxford   New York
Auckland   Cape Town   Dar es Salaam   Hong Kong   Karachi
Kuala Lumpur   Madrid   Melbourne   Mexico City   Nairobi
New Delhi   Shanghai   Taipei   Toronto

With offices in
Argentina   Austria   Brazil   Chile   Czech Republic   France   Greece
Guatemala   Hungary   Italy   Japan   Poland   Portugal   Singapore
South Korea   Switzerland   Thailand   Turkey   Ukraine   Vietnam

Copyright © 2012 by Oxford University Press, Inc.

Published by Oxford University Press, Inc.
198 Madison Avenue, New York, New York 10016
www.oup.com

Oxford is a registered trademark of Oxford University Press

All rights reserved. No part of this publication may be reproduced,
stored in a retrieval system, or transmitted, in any form or by any means,
electronic, mechanical, photocopying, recording, or otherwise,
without the prior permission of Oxford University Press.

Library of Congress Cataloging-in-Publication Data
Tausret : forgotten queen and pharaoh of Egypt / edited by Richard H. Wilkinson.
     p. cm.
Includes bibliographical references and index.
ISBN 978–0–19–974011–6
1. Tausret, Queen, consort of Seti II, King of Egypt, fl. ca. 1187–1185 B.C.   2. Queens—Egypt—
Biography.   3. Egypt—History—To 332 B.C.   4. Tausret, Queen, consort of Seti II, King of
Egypt, fl. ca. 1187-1185 B.C.—Tomb.   5. Tausret, Queen, consort of Seti II, King of Egypt, fl. ca.
1187–1185 B.C.—Monuments.   6. Egypt—Antiquities.   I. Wilkinson, Richard H.
DT87.T38 2011
932'.014092—dc22
[B]
                                        2011009267

9 8 7 6 5 4 3 2 1

Printed in the United States of America
on acid-free paper

Acknowledgments

The authors of this volume wish to thank the many individuals who have facilitated their research both in Egypt and in their own or other academic institutions. Specific acknowledgments are made in the notes to the individual chapters of the book, but the authors are all appreciative of the help provided by Oxford University Press.

The editor is particularly grateful to the authors for sharing their expertise on Pharaoh Tausret and for their diligence in making the present volume possible. In addition, his special thanks go to Justine Gesell for her translation of Chapter 4, and to his wife Anna for her constant help and encouragement. The editor would also like to thank Stefan Vranka for his interest and encouragement in this project, and all the OUP staff involved in bringing the volume to production.

Table of Contents

Contributors

Joyce Tyldesley

Lecturer in Egyptology, KNH Centre for Biomedical Egyptology, University of Manchester, and a Fellow of the Manchester Museum. Dr. Tyldesley is also Honorary Research Fellow at the School of Archaeology, Classics, and Egyptology at Liverpool University. She is the author of many works on ancient Egypt, including a number of studies of Egyptian women and ancient Egypt's queens including *Daughters of Isis: Women of Ancient Egypt, Hatchepsut: The Female Pharaoh, Nefertiti: Egypt's Sun Queen, Cleopatra: Last Queen of Egypt,* and *Chronicle of the Queens of Egypt.*

Gae Callender

Associate in Ancient History, School of History, Philosophy and Politics, Macquarie University, Australia. Dr. Callender has worked in Egypt at Abu Sir and elsewhere and is particularly interested in Egyptian queens and female royalty. She has focused a good deal of her research on the life and reign of Tausret and has published detailed studies such as "Queen Tausret and the End of Dynasty 19," *Studien zur Altägyptischen Kultur* 32 (2004): 81–104, as well as various books on Egypt and the surrounding ancient world.

Catharine H. Roehrig

Curator of Egyptian Art, Metropolitan Museum of Art, New York. Dr. Roehrig has extensive field experience in Egypt and has produced a number of Egyptological studies on the Valley of the Kings and its best known queen, Hatshepsut. She was one of the chief organizers of the Metropolitan Museum of Art's Hatshepsut Exhibition; and in this capacity she also served as editor and contributor to the important *Hatshepsut: From Queen to Pharaoh* (2006), which looks at both the historical background to that queen's reign and the known artifacts that have survived from it.

Hartwig Altenmüller

Emeritus Professor of Egyptian Archaeology, Archaeological Institute, University of Hamburg. Professor Altenmüller excavated in Saqqara from 1969 to 1982, and then in the Valley of the Kings from 1984 to 1998. Among his most important excavations, Altenmüller's work in the tomb of Tausret, and in related tombs such as KV13 where he discovered the queen's sarcophagus, make him the unparalleled expert in the funerary monument of Tausret. His many publications include formal studies of the queen's tomb (e.g., "Das Grab der Königin Tausret im Tal der Könige von Theben," *Studien zur Altägyptischen Kultur* 10 [1984]: 1–24.).

Richard H. Wilkinson

Regents' Professor of Egyptian Archaeology at the University of Arizona, Wilkinson directs the university's Egyptian Expedition and serves as editor of the *Journal of Ancient Egyptian Interconnections*. He has conducted research and excavation in and around the Valley of the Kings for a quarter of a century—including the excavation of Tausret's temple where numerous discoveries have added to our knowledge of the queen's reign. He is the author of many articles and nine previous books on Egyptology (with more than twenty translations), including *The Complete Valley of the Kings* and *The Complete Temples of Ancient Egypt* for Thames & Hudson. Professor Wilkinson has edited three previous volumes, *Valley of the Sun Kings* and *The Temple of Tausret* for the University of Arizona and *Egyptology Today* for Cambridge University Press.

Chronology of the New Kingdom

This chronology is based partly on that given in Ian Shaw, ed. *The Oxford History of Ancient Egypt* (Oxford: Oxford University Press, 2000). Monarchs are identified by their cartouche names: first the ruler's birth name and then, parenthetically, the throne name. Dates given are approximate in some cases, and all are subject to ongoing study of the chronology of New Kingdom Egypt.

Dynasty 18

Ahmose	(Nebpehtyra)	1550–1525
Amenhotep I	(Djeserkara)	1525–1504
Thutmose I	(Aakheperkara)	1504–1492
Thutmose II	(Aakheperenra)	1492–1479
Thutmose III	(Menkheperra)	1479–1425
Hatshepsut	(Maatkara)	1473–1458
Amenhotep II	(Aakheperura)	1427–1400
Thutmose IV	(Menkheperura)	1400–1390
Amenhotep III	(Nebmaatra)	1390–1352
Amenhotep IV/ Akhenaten	(Neferkheperura Waenra)	1352–1336
Smenkhkara	(Ankhkheperura)	1338–1336
Tutankhamen	(Nebkheperura)	1336–1327
Aye	(Kheperkheperura)	1327–1323
Horemheb	(Djeserkheperura)	1323–1295

Dynasty 19

Ramesses I	(Menpehtyra)	1295–1294
Sety I	(Menmaatra)	1294–1279
Ramesses II	(Usermaatra Setepenra)	1279–1213
Merenptah	(Baenra Hotephermaat)	1213–1203
Amenmesse	(Menmira)	1203–1200?
Sety II	(Userkheperura Setepenra)	1200–1194
Siptah	(Akhenra Setepenra)	1194–1188
Tausret	(Sitra Merytamen)	1188–1186?

Dynasty 20

Sethnakht	(Userkhaura Meryamen)	1186–1184?
Ramesses III	(Usermaatra Meryamen)	1184–1153
Ramesses IV	(Hekamaatra Setepenamen)	1153–1147
Ramesses V	(Usermaatra Sekheperenra)	1147–1143
Ramesses VI	(Nebmaatra Meryamen)	1143–1136
Ramesses VII	(Usermaatra Setepenra Merytamen)	1136–1129
Ramesses VIII	(Usermaatra Akhenamen)	1129–1126
Ramesses IX	(Neferkara Setepenra)	1126–1108
Ramesses X	(Khepermaatra Setepenra)	1108–1099
Ramesses XI	(Menmaatra Setepenptah)	1099–1069

Introduction

The Queen Who Would Be King

RICHARD H. WILKINSON

Until very recently the name of the ancient Egyptian queen Tausret (*Ta-Usret* "The Powerful One" and also spelled Tausert, Taousert, Twosret, Tawosret, etc.) was known only to trained Egyptologists and to lovers of ancient Egyptian culture who read deeply in the history and archaeology of this great civilization of the past. Today, as marked by this book, the situation is changing quickly. Once a truly forgotten queen, whose name meant nothing in comparison to those of Hatshepsut and Cleopatra VII, recent research has led to a greater understanding of the times and reign of this woman who ruled her country at the time of Homer's Troy—as queen, as regent, and then as pharaoh.

Ancient Egyptian religious beliefs dictated that the pharaoh was the "*son* of the sun god" and that the person of the living king also represented the god Horus. Because of this theological underpinning of Egyptian monarchical ideology, at least from the religious perspective, female pharaohs theoretically could not exist. This was usually evident in practice, but over the more than three thousand years of Egyptian history a very few women—through circumstances or personal power or ambition—did ascend the throne and rule as pharaohs. Sometimes this situation occurred at the end of dynastic lines when male heirs were absent or when they were infirm or underage. Nevertheless, the importance of these female rulers is evident, and their reigns were all the more important for their situation at pivotal times of dynastic transition or change. Thus, Cleopatra VII is as well known for the events and policies of her own reign as for the fact that she ruled at the end of the Ptolemaic dynasty and the beginning of Roman rule in Egypt. The female pharaoh Tausret is historically important in a similar if far less well-documented manner. Tausret ruled at a time of dynastic change during Egypt's powerful New Kingdom period. She ruled first as chief queen of the pharaoh Sety II, then as regent during the reign of his young son, Siptah, and finally as pharaoh in her own right for several years after the death of Siptah. Yet very little has been known of the life and reign of this queen, as the historical situation in which she ruled has long been unclear[1] and is only now becoming somewhat more firmly established. The growth in our knowledge has not been quick or easy. As recently as the second half of the twentieth century there was very little understanding of who this woman was and what she had accomplished in relation to some of the other rulers of the late 19th Dynasty. Indeed, as late as 1958 the celebrated English Egyptologist Sir Alan Gardiner published an article titled "Only One King Siptah and Twosre Not His Wife,"[2] correcting fundamental misunderstandings that were still common little more than fifty years ago.

The process of recovering the historical Tausret has been recently enhanced not through the discovery of some previously unknown archaeological site or hidden trove of ancient texts, however, but through a great many hours of excavation, study, and research in which sometimes even small and unassuming facts and artifacts have been brought together to shed light on a mysterious queen whose reign has long been obscured by the shadows of time. Although a detailed and widely documented treatment of the queen's life is still not possible in the same way that it is for Cleopatra VII, for example, this book brings together scholars whose research and excavations have increased our understanding of Tausret's era and have demonstrated the importance of the queen, despite her long-standing position as a nearly forgotten female pharaoh.

Tausret ruled Egypt for a number of years from shortly after 1200 BCE (scholarly estimates vary and range from 1209 to 1185 BCE as the beginning of her reign). Far from being a transient pretender to the throne, she appears to have been universally accepted as ruler, and there is no question that her rule embraced all of Egypt. Artifacts bearing her name have also been found at sites distant from Egypt; expeditions seem to have been dispatched to the turquoise mines of Sinai during the queen's reign; and her name has been found on items discovered as far away as Lebanon to the north and Nubia in the south. Research on the queen's temple has shown that she probably reigned longer than we had previously thought, although eventually Tausret was either overthrown by or succeeded upon her death by Sethnakht, founder of Egypt's 20th Dynasty.

During her reign, Tausret seems to have repeatedly stressed her relationship to her famous predecessor Ramesses II—Ramesses the Great; indeed, she may have been his granddaughter. Her royal cartouche names were carefully contrived as visual simulacrums of those of Ramesses, with some of the elements changed only slightly to make them feminine. Her statuary—at least in one known case—closely copied that of Ramesses, and we know now that even her temple copied the interior plan of that of Ramesses, the great Ramesseum. In patterning elements of her reign on those of Ramesses, was she displaying the mark of a woman who had little claim to the throne and who desperately sought legitimization, or evidence of a strong-willed woman who rallied her country behind ancient ideals at a time of national decline? We may not know the answers to such basic questions, but we do know far more about the queen than we did only a decade or so ago. Scholarly interest in this female pharaoh has begun to expand, and various aspects of her reign and monuments are now coming under increasingly focused study.[3]

The following chapters were written by experts who, in one way or another, have been involved in the development of our present understanding of Egyptian regnal queens and of Tausret in particular. The chapters summarize the research of recent years—up to 2011—and present its conclusions and our present knowledge of the pharaoh-queen in an ordered manner ranging from the position of her reign in its broader historical setting to what is known of the woman herself and the details of her known artifacts and monuments.

Chapter 1, "Foremost of Women: The Female Pharaohs of Ancient Egypt," examines the broader context in which Tausret's life and reign must be understood by examining the positions and roles of royal women in Egypt—focusing on the known queens who ruled in their own names—from earliest times till Cleopatra VII. Beyond its biographical analysis, this chapter examines areas of connection between ancient Egypt's female pharaohs by considering underlying questions such as "What were the factors that affected female rule and how did these factors affect the kind of situation in which Tausret became pharaoh?"

Chapter 2, "Female Horus: The Life and Reign of Tausret," examines the immediate historical context of Tausret's life and situates her within that understanding as well as illuminating the queen's reign by facts gleaned from recent archaeological discoveries. Beginning with Tausret's unique literary-historic role as Egypt's pharaoh at the time of the Trojan War, her apparent appearance in Homer's *Odyssey* is sketched before the details we have of her reign are considered. Both the uniqueness of the queen's reign and the similarities between Tausret and other female rulers are examined. The special position of Tausret as the last ruling descendent of Ramesses the Great is explored in detail, as we now know that this was a vital part of the queen's program of legitimation and an important aspect in understanding her monuments.

Chapter 3, "Forgotten Treasures: Tausret as Seen in Her Monuments," looks at the scattered and sometimes enigmatic artifacts that have survived from the reign of Tausret—ranging from small items of jewelry found in the Valley of the Kings to larger two- and three- dimensional representations of the queen. Together, these artifacts and representations provide images of Tausret, or other clues, which may be analyzed in terms of their historical context or how they portray the queen and what this portrayal may tell us of the way she chose to be depicted.

Chapter 4, "A Queen in a Valley of Kings: The Tomb of Tausret," explores the tomb of Tausret (KV-14), one of the largest and most interesting monuments in the Valley of the Kings, and one that is key to much of our understanding of the queen's reign. Careful study of the history and decoration of this tomb by its excavator—as well as the nearby tomb of Chancellor Bay, in whose tomb the queen's sarcophagus was found—has shown a complex development that occurred over time, beginning with Tausret as queen and regent, then as pharaoh, and then, finally, as a monarch deposed or succeeded by Sethnakht, first ruler of the 20th Dynasty. The massive and extensively decorated tomb not only allows us to trace the history of the queen's reign but also holds clues to the nature of the queen's legitimation and evidence of her final demise.

Chapter 5, "The 'Temple of Millions of Years' of Tausret," looks at the most recently recovered archaeological evidence for the queen—that of the temple she founded close to the temple of her illustrious ancestor, Ramesses the Great. The temple was supposedly excavated by the great English archaeologist Sir William Flinders Petrie, who concluded that the site held little more than foundations for the structure. Research conducted over the last eight years has shown, however, that the site was not actually explored beyond a very cursory probing by Petrie's men. The recent work has uncovered not only thousands of small artifacts but also important inscriptions, and clear evidence that the temple was probably completed in ancient times and doubtless played an important role in Tausret's quest for immortality through her personal monument.

As these chapters demonstrate, we still have many questions—often at the most fundamental levels—regarding the life, reign, and monuments of Tausret. However, the inscriptions, as well as clear evidence, that we now have allows us to begin to paint a picture of a fascinating woman who was as good as lost from history due to our lack of information—and sometimes the effects of disinformation. Now Tausret can be more clearly seen as an important figure in Egyptian history by virtue of her role as one of only a very few women who, in over three thousand years, ascended and ruled from the Horus throne of the pharaohs.

I

Foremost of Women: The Female Pharaohs of Ancient Egypt

JOYCE TYLDESLEY

To appreciate the life and reign of Tausret, and to set her in her proper social and historical context, it is necessary to understand the unique role allocated to the principal royal women—the queen consorts and queen mothers—of ancient Egypt. This chapter considers the historical and archaeological evidence for their lives, paying particular attention to the select group of women who could claim the title "female pharaoh."

The Women of Ancient Egypt

Abundant natural resources made Egypt a very wealthy country. Yet with no efficient health care and no official welfare program, life was both brief and insecure for many, and the family offered the only reliable protection against uncertainties. Marriage created an economic unit to support both husband and wife during their lifetime; their children would, it was hoped, support them in death by making the necessary funerary offerings. Everyone therefore expected to marry, and girls were raised to become good wives and mothers.[1]

Egyptian law treated men and women of equivalent social status as equals. Women could own, buy, sell, and inherit property. They could bring cases before the law courts and could be punished by them. And they could act as deputies for their husbands in business matters. This was unusual by the standards of the Classical world, but less so in comparison to neighboring Near

Eastern societies.[2] Women, and mothers in particular, were respected, but it would be naive to assume that husbands did not assume the right to control their households. The Old Kingdom scribe Ptahhotep offered his schoolboy readers some good advice in this respect: "Do not argue with your wife in court. Keep her from power—restrain her....In this way you will make her stay in your home."[3]

Married couples led very different lives, performing complementary but opposite roles. While the "Mistress of the House" assumed responsibility for domestic matters, her husband worked outside the home. This allocation of duties is reflected in the artistic convention that presented women as pale beings beside their more weather-beaten, darker-skinned husbands. Poorer women, and unmarried women, might also work outside the home, but few if any women (and, indeed, few men) received the education that would allow a professional career. As their traditional duties of child care, cooking, and laundry have had little impact on the archaeological record, these illiterate women tend to be invisible to us. This bias in evidence is made worse by a shortage of domestic sites, as most of Egypt's mud-brick palaces, cities, and villages have been lost. Only a few, highly atypical, women have been able to leave evidence of their lives. Included among these are the queens who ruled Egypt as kings.

From the very beginning of the dynastic age in approximately 3100 BCE, to its end in 30 BCE, Egypt was ruled by a king, or pharaoh.[4] Pharaoh was the one Egyptian who could serve as a link between the people and their pantheon; the only living person who could make the regular offerings that the gods craved. In consequence, to pharaoh fell the responsibility of maintaining *maat*: the ideal state of affairs within Egypt.[5] This was an onerous and awesome burden. Pharaoh was required to officiate in the temples, to rule in the law courts, and to fight off any enemies—either foreigners or criminals—who might disrupt the status quo. Thus, and only thus, would *maat* be preserved. With *maat* in place, the gods would be happy and the land would prosper; with *maat* absent, chaos would flood the land and Egypt would fail. This overwhelming need to preserve *maat* was responsible for the innate conservatism of the ancient Egyptians. Any deviation from tradition—and, in particular, any threat to the monarchy—was seen as a potential threat to *maat*.[6]

It was therefore vital that there was always a pharaoh on the Egyptian throne. The ideal pharaoh would be the son of the previous king. He would be youthful yet mature, healthy, brave, and wise; essentially, he would be the continuation of all successful pharaohs who had gone before. However, it was not always possible to meet this ideal. Occasionally a pharaoh came to the throne as an old man, or as an infant or a commoner. Some pharaohs were ill or infirm (although they did their best to hide this in their official propaganda).[7]

And although the overwhelming majority were male, a very few were female. None of that mattered. Once pharaoh had undergone the correct coronation rituals he, or she, acquired a veneer of divinity that would allow him, or her, to function as a proper king. This partial divinity would remain in place until death transformed pharaoh into a fully divine being.

Technically, then, a woman might become pharaoh.[8] But that would happen only if there was no more suitable male candidate for the throne and, given that the royal harem usually produced multiple sons, that was a relatively rare event. Just three female pharaohs—the 12th-Dynasty Sobekneferu, 18th-Dynasty Hatshepsut, and 19th-Dynasty Tausret—are universally accepted as having ruled pre-Ptolemaic Egypt in their own right, although various authorities have proposed several others. These three reigns were undertaken at very different times and in very different circumstances. Nevertheless, it is possible to draw some broad parallels. All three women were of royal birth, each either the daughter or granddaughter of a king, and each apparently served as queen-consort before becoming pharaoh. None had a living son to succeed her.

Each male pharaoh needed a wife by his side. Egypt's queen-consort provided the feminine element of the semi-divine monarchy, supporting the king and performing female-based religious duties.[9] But every pharaoh also had a mother who, by having given birth to a quasi-divine being, was herself touched with divinity. While the king and queen created a partnership strong enough to confound chaos, the king and his mother formed a second, unbreakable partnership. At the same time, the dowager-queen and the queen-consort were linked by their shared duty to protect pharaoh. Their relative importance alternated as the dynastic age progressed, with first the king's wife, and then the king's mother, holding the most important role in the royal family.

Egypt's Queens

In the English language a "king" is always a male ruler, while a "queen" can be either the wife or widow of a king, or a monarch ruling in her own right. But in ancient Egypt, where royal titles invariably stressed relationships to the pharaoh, the queen's title *ḥmt nswt*, which was used from the 4th Dynasty onward, literally meant "king's wife." So an Egyptian queen was by definition a woman who was, or had been, married to a king. Women who ruled Egypt in their own right classed themselves as female pharaohs, or kings.

As pharaohs maintained increasingly large harems, there were many, many king's wives; it is difficult to give precise numbers, but it is likely that the three hundred or so pharaohs generated several thousand women entitled to use the title queen. The most important of these were the queen-consorts: the queens at the heart of the royal family whose sons were expected to inherit the throne. These women were distinguished from lesser queens by an increasingly elaborate series of crowns and titles. They had a recognized political and religious role, were represented in official writings and artwork, and were buried in splendid tombs. From the Middle Kingdom onward, they wrote their names in cartouches. Eventually they would become the next "King's Mother." They might even rule Egypt, temporarily, on behalf of an absent husband or an infant son.

In some periods, many queen-consorts were the full- or half-sister of the king. To a people unaware of hereditary diseases, these unions brought several practical benefits. They ensured that the queen was well prepared for her role and that she was loyal to her husband rather than her birth family. They reduced the number of potential claimants to the throne by restricting the number of royal grandchildren, and they provided a link with the gods who had enjoyed incestuous marriages. However, brother-sister marriages were by no means compulsory.[10]

The king's lesser wives spent much of their lives in harem palaces—communities built to house the king's female dependents plus their children and servants. These harem queens were by no means of equal status. Some were the daughters of Egyptian kings, some were foreign princesses sent by their fathers to make diplomatic marriages, and some were women of relatively humble birth.

Queens of the Early Dynastic Period (Dynasties 1 and 2, c. 3000–2686 BCE)

We know little of Egypt's first queens beyond their names, which are often compounded with that of the ancient creator Neith. A far from passive goddess, Neith was a hunter and a warrior whose prowess with the bow was reflected in her emblem of crossed bows or crossed arrows.[11] Neithhotep has been identified as the wife of the first pharaoh, Narmer, and therefore as Egypt's first queen. She bore the titles "Consort of the Two Ladies" and "Foremost of Women," and occasionally wrote her name in a *serekh* (the rectangular box representing the royal palace that was invariably drawn around the names of the earliest pharaohs) topped with the crossed arrows of Neith.[12] This assumption of a pharaoh's protocol suggests that Neithhotep may have ruled Egypt temporarily on behalf of her son Aha. This is a situation that we will encounter time and time again: when an infant inherits the throne, it is his mother who acts on his behalf until he is old enough to assume his duties. But as the queen's temporary "reign" falls entirely within that of her son, it may prove impossible for modern historians to detect.

While the pharaohs of the 1st Dynasty were interred in the royal cemetery at Abydos, their consorts were buried elsewhere. Just one consort was accorded the honor of burial among the kings. Meritneith, consort of Djet, mother of Den and (probable) daughter of Djer, was interred in Tomb Y.[13] Meritneith occasionally uses the *serekh* and this, combined with the fact that she was probably included on a broken section of the Palermo Stone (a record of the kings of Dynasties 1–5), suggests that she too ruled on behalf of her son. We may therefore regard her splendid tomb, set among the tombs of her fellow rulers, as a reward for her reign.[14]

There were, however, some lesser queens buried beside the 1st-Dynasty kings. Each royal tomb was surrounded by a series of satellite graves whose shared roof suggests that they were provided for subjects or relatives who were expected, maybe even forced, to die when pharaoh died.[15] The earlier tombs had large numbers of these subsidiary graves—Djer had over 300—but the tradition gradually dwindled away and is not found in the 2nd Dynasty. The dead were buried in short wooden coffins, and their names and a few titles were preserved on small stelae carved by the royal workshop. While some of these stelae are unreadable, it is clear that the vast majority belonged to women, and it seems likely that they represent pharaoh's closest courtiers, including his harem wives.[16]

Queens of the Old Kingdom (Dynasties 3–8, c. 2686–2125 BCE)

The pyramid-building pharaohs of the Old Kingdom considered themselves to be both the living Horus and the son of the solar god Re. From the 4th Dynasty onward their consorts and mothers were equated with Hathor, a solar goddess who had a double link with the Horus king as she could be either the wife of the adult Horus or the protective mother-cow who nourished the infant Horus and, by extension, suckled and protected all of Egypt's pharaohs. A series of triads recovered from the Giza mortuary temple of Menkaure show the king and Hathor standing with various local deities: Hathor invariably wears a sheath dress and a headdress of cow horns and a solar disk. A contemporary dyad of Menkaure and an unnamed woman, conventionally identified as his consort Kharmerernebty II but possibly his mother, Kharmerernebty I, shows the queen looking nearly identical to Hathor but lacking the goddess's diagnostic headdress.[17]

Goddesses had always worn distinguishing crowns. Now queens, too, were starting to develop their own regalia. First to appear was the vulture crown, a headdress that resembled a bird draped over the wearer's head, with the body forming a cap, the wings hanging at the sides of the face, and the vulture's head and neck rising from the forehead. This was originally the headdress worn by Nekhbet, vulture goddess of southern Egypt and, in some mythologies, mother of the king. Other goddesses subsequently adopted it, while Wadjet, cobra goddess of northern Egypt, replaced the bird's head with a uraeus (rearing cobra). This modified vulture headdress would be worn by consorts from the 6th Dynasty onward, emphasizing the link both between the queen and motherhood (vultures and snakes being considered good mothers) and between the queen and the uraeus-wearing pharaoh. The simple vulture headdress, too, would become a standard part of the queen's regalia, but during the 4th Dynasty it may have been reserved for the dowager-queen.

The increasing use of stone throughout the Old Kingdom allows us to see that queens were often depicted at a much smaller scale than their husbands. In Egyptian art, where size always mattered, this was a reflection of the consort's (and, indeed, the wife's) status relative to that of the husband who commissioned the image. The first miniature queen is the 3rd-Dynasty Hetephernebty, who appears on a fragment of a smashed stone shrine standing beside the leg of her gigantic husband, Djoser.[18] This difference in size was not inevitable: the Menkaure dyad already discussed shows the king and queen at a similar scale. Nor need queens always appear with a husband: the so-called Galarza tomb at Giza has yielded a series of statues including a colossal Kharmerernebty II.[19]

Although we have most of the burial equipment of Hetepheres (Figure 1.1, see insert), mother of the 4th-Dynasty pharaoh Khufu, we know little of her life.[20] It is not until the early 5th Dynasty that we find our first politically prominent queen. Khentkawes I is the owner of an extensive, two-stepped pyramid-mastaba tomb at Giza[21] The titles carved on the doorway to her mortuary temple include an ambiguous phrase that can be translated as either "Mother of Two Kings of Upper and Lower Egypt," or "King of Upper and Lower Egypt and Mother of the King of Upper and Lower Egypt." Initially Egyptologists accepted the first interpretation, believing that Khentkawes had given birth to two kings, Sahure and Neferirkare, the second and third kings of the 5th Dynasty. However, Miroslav Verner has recently suggested that an image carved on Khentkawes' doorjamb shows her sitting on a throne, wearing a false beard and uraeus and carrying a scepter. This image is, unfortunately, faint and unclear. Khentkawes' name is never found in a cartouche, but if Verner is correct, it would seem that she too served as a temporary monarch.[22]

The entirely fictional Papyrus Westcar tells the story of the triplet sons of Re, born to the lady Redjedet.[23] The babies are addressed by the midwife Isis: "Do not be so strong in your mother's womb, you whose name means Strong" (a pun on the name Userkaf); "do not kick in your mother's womb, you whose name means Kicker" (Sahure); "do not be dark in your mother's womb, you whose name means Dark" (Neferirkare Kakai). This is far from accurate history, but it does link Redjedet (a corruption of Khentkawes?) with the first three kings of the 5th Dynasty: Userkaf, Sahure, and Nyuserre. Userkaf, founder of the 5th Dynasty, is a man of unknown but presumably royal origins and it seems likely that he was married to Khentkawes I. As Userkaf reigned for just eight years, it is possible that his heir, Sahure, would have needed his mother's guidance. However, the situation becomes more complicated when we consider the evidence from the Abusir pyramid complex of Khentkawes II, consort to Neferirkare.[24] Here, included among entirely conventional images, we see Khentkawes wearing a uraeus and using the same ambiguous title "Mother of Two Kings of Upper and Lower Egypt" or "King of Upper and Lower Egypt and Mother of the King of Upper and Lower Egypt." Although Khentkawes I and II may be the same woman, it is generally accepted that they are separate, identically named queens. Khentkawes I seems to have ruled Egypt on behalf of at least one son. Whether Khentkawes II also ruled on behalf of a son or was simply the mother of two kings (Neferefre and Nyuserre) is not obvious.

Herodotus tells us that Nitocris, last queen of the 6th Dynasty, succeeded her murdered brother to the throne.[25] Determined to avenge him, she built an underground banqueting chamber. Having invited her brother's assassins to a feast, she opened a conduit to the river. When all the murderers had drowned, Nitocris committed suicide rather than explain her actions to her people. This dramatic, and highly un-Egyptian, story is unlikely to be true. Nitocris has left neither monument nor tomb, and although the 19th-Dynasty Turin Canon allocates the otherwise unknown "Neitaqerti" a reign of two years, one month, and one day, it seems probable that "Neitaqerti" is a misrecorded male name.

Queens of the Middle Kingdom (Dynasties 11–13, c. 2055–1650 BCE)

While the Middle Kingdom pharaohs reestablished the traditions of their Old Kingdom predecessors, adopting their propaganda, regalia, and burial customs, their consorts, denied the prominence accorded to the Old Kingdom queens, had little impact on state affairs and all but vanished from the royal monuments. This phenomenon was not restricted to the royal family, and it is clear that relatively few elite women bore priestly titles.[26] Our knowledge of the Middle Kingdom queens is therefore largely restricted to their names, their tombs, and their surviving grave goods. During the 12th Dynasty we find the introduction of the title "King's Great Wife," a title that helps us to distinguish the consort from lesser queens.[27]

The tradition of female reticence came to an abrupt end during the reign of the 12th-Dynasty pharaoh Amenemhat III. Amenemhat was a dynamic and prosperous monarch, yet his death heralded the collapse of his dynasty. Evidence from his Hawara pyramid suggests that his failure to produce a satisfactory male heir may have been a contributing factor to this collapse. Included in his burial chamber was a wooden coffin for "the King's Daughter Ptahnofru." It seems that Ptahnofru, having died unexpectedly, had to be temporarily interred in her father's tomb to allow the builders sufficient time to complete her pyramid.[28] Ptahnofru's use of a cartouche in her later inscriptions suggests that she had been her father's intended successor. Instead, with Ptahnofru already dead, Amenemhat IV briefly succeeded Amenemhat III.

Amenemhat IV was in turn succeeded as pharaoh by his half-sister and probable consort Sobekneferu. Sobekneferu never explains her elevation to the throne but she does emphasize her hereditary right to rule by consistently associating herself with her father Amenemhat III: she may even have been the first to deify Amenemhat III in the Faiyum. The fact that later historians were happy to incorporate her in their king lists indicates that she was always regarded as a legitimate pharaoh.

Three badly damaged statues of Sobekneferu have been recovered from the Delta site of Avaris; we may assume that these originated in the Faiyum where Sobekneferu ruled the whole of Egypt from the (now lost) city of Idj-Tawi. The most interesting of these pieces is headless and limbless. Carved from red quartzite, it shows the queen's female body dressed in an awkward combination of queen's and king's clothing: a female shift dress with a royal kilt tied over the top.[29] On her head Sobekneferu wears a king's *nemes* head cloth; her titles are inscribed on her belt. An equally damaged schist statue shows her wearing a king's ritual cloak.[30] Without in any way denying her gender—she almost invariably uses feminine titles—Sobekneferu is here allowing herself to be depicted in the traditional regalia that will reinforce her role as pharaoh. In other images she is entirely female in appearance, but she assumes a male pose to perform the ritual of trampling Egypt's enemies.

The Turin Canon allows Sobekneferu a reign of three years, ten months, and twenty-four days. Her pyramid has never been identified.

Sobekneferu's Names as Ruler

Horus name: *Meryt-Re*
Nebty name: *Sat-Sekhem Nebet-Tawy*
Golden Horus name: *Djedet-Khaw*
Prenomen/King of Upper and Lower Egypt: *Ka-Sobek-Re*
Nomen: *Sobek-Nofru*
Horus name: Beloved of Re
Nebty name: Powerful Daughter, Mistress of the Two Lands.
Golden Horus name: Rising in Stability
Prenomen/King of Upper and Lower Egypt: Sobek is the soul of Re
Nomen: Sobekneferu [the Beauties of Sobek]

Queens of the Earlier 18th Dynasty (c. 1550–1390 BCE)

As the Theban pharaohs of the late 17th Dynasty started the long fight to reunite their land, their consorts were required to take supportive action in the absence of their husbands and sons. An increased emphasis on, and respect for, the individuality of each consort allowed their deeds to be recorded, and this allows us to recognize different personalities in a way that has been impossible before.[31]

Tetisheri, consort of Sekenenre Taa I, was a formidable queen. She would be remembered with such respect by her grandson Ahmose, founder of the 18th Dynasty, that he built an elaborate cenotaph for her in the Abydos cemetery. Even greater was the respect that Ahmose felt for his mother Ahhotep I, consort of Seqenenre Taa II and daughter of Tetisheri. Ahhotep had raised Ahmose and his sister-consort Ahmose-Nefertari following the death of his father in battle. On a stela erected at Karnak, Ahmose boasted that his mother performed the rites, guarded Egypt, and cared for Egypt's soldiers.[32] Ahhotep's successful defense of her land (Thebes, rather than the whole of Egypt) explains why her coffin included, along with the expected jewelry, an inscribed ceremonial axe, a gold dagger and sheath, and three golden flies: the "medals" awarded to successful soldiers.[33]

The New Kingdom consorts maintained the high status inherited from their late 17th-Dynasty predecessors, adopting increasing numbers of secular and religious titles and an expanded range of crowns and headdresses that now included the double uraeus. Hathor and Isis wore similar crowns so that, at a time when many pharaohs were hinting at their own earthly divinity, their queens and their goddesses appeared almost interchangeable. This increase in status coincided with an expansion in the size of the royal harem. The New Kingdom kings—now the richest and most powerful rulers in the Mediterranean world—married many, many times. While foreign princesses traveled to Egypt to marry pharaoh (several princesses marrying each king), there was no reciprocal exchange of brides. From the late 17th Dynasty until the mid-19th we have no evidence of any Egyptian princess marrying anyone other than an Egyptian king.

Ahmose-Nefertari proved a worthy successor to her mother. Alongside her standard royal titles "King's Daughter," "King's Sister," and "King's Great Wife"—she became "Second Priest of Amun" and was simultaneously both "Divine Adoratrice" and "God's Wife of Amun." The income generated from these lucrative positions allowed her to make generous offerings to the gods, and her name has been recorded in temples at Abydos, Thebes, and Serabit el-Khadim in Sinai. She is also recorded, in association with her husband, in the limestone quarries and alabaster quarries. When Ahmose died, Ahmose-Nefertari served as regent for their young son, Amenhotep I. Later, following the death of his childless sister-wife Meritamen, she acted as Amenhotep's consort. Dying during the reign of Thutmose I, she was buried in the Dra Abu el-Naga cemetery on the Theban west bank. But that was not the end of her story. Amenhotep I and Ahmose-Nefertari had become so closely linked that both were deified as patrons of the workmen's village of Deir el-Medina. Here Ahmose-Nefertari was worshipped as a goddess of resurrection until the end of the New Kingdom.

Egypt's next pharaoh was the commoner-born Thutmose I. His consort, Ahmose, used the title "King's Sister" but was apparently not a king's daughter. She bore her husband two daughters but no son. Ahmose remained in the background during her husband's reign and the subsequent reign of her stepson, Thutmose II, only to be given a prominent role in the divine birth story of her daughter, the female pharaoh Hatshepsut.

Following the death of Thutmose I, Hatshepsut became consort and "God's Wife of Amun" to her half brother, Thutmose II. She bore a daughter, Neferure, but not a son, and so, when Thutmose II died, the throne passed to the infant Thutmose III, a son born to the harem queen Isis. As the new king needed an experienced queen to help him reign, Hatshepsut stepped forward and assumed the title "Mistress of the Two Lands." Initially this was a conventional regency, although Hatshepsut's commissioning of a pair of obelisks for the Karnak temple of Amun hints at her unusual ambition. Then, some time before her stepson's Regnal Year 7, Hatshepsut was crowned pharaoh. In a throwback to Middle Kingdom tradition, she ruled as the dominant king alongside the now junior Thutmose III.[34]

Hatshepsut now needed to present herself as a traditional pharaoh. We don't know how she dressed in real life, but her earlier images and statuary show her either as a conventional woman or as a woman wearing king's clothing, while her later art shows her as a stereotypical king with a male body dressed in male clothing. Her monumental texts are less consistent, and she alternates between the feminine and masculine forms of her titulary (Figure 1.2, see insert).

Like many modern politicians, Hatshepsut neither explains nor apologizes for her actions. We may speculate that she acted because Egypt was threatened by a situation requiring a fully adult pharaoh, but there is no evidence of any political, military, or religious crisis at this time. It may simply be that she felt, as the daughter, sister, and wife of a pharaoh, that her contribution to maintaining the monarchy should be recognized. There is no indication that anyone opposed her elevation, and we must assume that she had the support of the elite who effectively ran the priesthood, civil service, and army. Nor is there any evidence that anyone—not even Thutmose III—ever attempted to remove her from power. Once she had completed the coronation rituals, she remained pharaoh until her death. She does, however, offer us some justification. She is entitled to rule because she is the true heir of Thutmose I and so, like Sobekneferu before her, she consistently links herself to her powerful and widely revered father. At the same time she is the semi-divine "Daughter of

Hatshepsut's Names as Ruler

Horus name: *Usert-Kaw*
Nebty name: *Wadjet-Renput*
Golden Horus name: *Netjeret-Khaw*
Prenomen/King of Upper and Lower Egypt: *Maatkare*
Nomen: *Khenmet-Amun Hatshepsut*
Horus name: Powerful-of-*Kas*
Nebty name: Flourishing-of-Years
Golden Horus name: Divine-of-Diadems
Prenomen/King of Upper and Lower Egypt: Maat is the Soul of Re
Nomen: The One who is joined with Amun, the Foremost of Women

Amun." And he, via an oracle, has proclaimed his daughter pharaoh. The tale of Hatshepsut's divine conception and birth is told in words and pictures on the walls of her Theban temple.

Hatshepsut inherited her late brother's advisors and then, as her reign developed, promoted new courtiers, many of whom were self-made men of relatively humble birth. But male advisors were not enough. Every pharaoh needed a wife or, occasionally, a mother, who could fulfill the female-based ritual aspects of the kingship. For this, Hatshepsut turned to her daughter Neferure, and for a time we see her serving as "Lady of Upper and Lower Egypt," "Mistress of the Lands," and "God's Wife of Amun." Neferure disappeared toward the end of her mother's reign and we must assume that she died young.

Having committed one extraordinary act, Hatshepsut embarked on an entirely typical reign dedicated to the maintenance of *maat*. A token series of military campaigns to the south and east ensured that all foreign rebels were successfully subdued. Then, with no more enemies to fight, Hatshepsut turned her attention to international trade. There were missions to Lebanon, increased exploitation of the copper and turquoise mines, and during Year 9, a spectacularly successful trading mission to the land of Punt.

There was probably a temple-building project in every major city. We know that Hatshepsut built in Nubia, Kom Ombo, Hierakonpolis, el-Kab, Armant, Elephantine, and Middle Egypt, where the rock-cut temple known today as the Speos Artemidos was dedicated to Pakhet, a local variant of Sekhmet (Hathor). But with most of these temples lost, it is her Theban monuments that stand as testament to the prosperity of Hatshepsut's reign. The Karnak temple was endowed with another pair of obelisks, a boat shrine (the Red Chapel), a new pylon, and improved processional routes. A new royal palace accommodated Hatshepsut as she performed the necessary rituals. On the west bank, Hatshepsut built a tiered, rock-cut temple in the Deir el-Bahri bay.[35] This was a multi-functional complex. The main sanctuary, on the highest tier, was dedicated to Amun, but there was also a suite of chapels for the royal ancestors which included a chapel for Thutmose I and a much larger chapel for Hatshepsut herself. On the same level an open-air court was dedicated to the sun god Re-Herakhty, while on a lower level there were chapels for Anubis and to Hathor, goddess of the Deir el-Bahri bay and "Mistress of Punt."

Rather than build a new tomb in the Valley of the Kings, Hatshepsut enlarged her father's tomb (KV 20) until it became the longest and deepest in the Valley. Here, following her death on the tenth day of the sixth month of Year 22, father and daughter lay together until Thutmose III had his grandfather re-interred in KV 38.[36] With Hatshepsut dead, Thutmose ruled alone for a further thirty-three years. Toward the end of his reign an attempt was made to delete all obvious references to Hatshepsut as pharaoh. Her cartouches and images were chiseled off walls and her statues were pulled down. Her reign was excluded from the official history that now ran directly from Thutmose II to Thutmose III. For many years Egyptologists assumed that it was a *damnatio memoriae*, the deliberate erasure of a dead person's memory that would cause the individual to die a second death in the Afterlife. But this is almost certainly too simple an explanation, and there is no evidence to suggest that Thutmose hated his co-ruler. It seems more likely that Thutmose was, toward the end of his life, simply relegating Hatshepsut to what he perceived as her rightful place as a queen who enjoyed temporary rule rather than as a female pharaoh.

The solo reign of Thutmose III brought a slight decline in the prominence allowed to royal women. While queens continued to be associated with goddesses, consorts were no longer routinely chosen from among the king's sisters, suggesting perhaps that pharaohs may have become reluctant to allow their close female relatives too much power. Only king's mothers—women who posed little threat to ruling sons—retained and even increased their former position. Tia, consort of Amenhotep II, is a good example of this new type of queen. A relatively obscure figure during her husband's reign, Tia achieved prominence during the reign of her son, Thutmose IV, when she served as "God's Wife." The close bond between mother and son was emphasized in inscriptions suggesting that Tia was the earthly counterpart of Hathor, Isis, and Mut, wife of Amun. Similarly Mutemwia, mother of Amenhotep III, never served as consort and we know nothing of her life until her son's reign, when she featured in the story of his divine birth as the child of Amun.

Queens of the Later 18th Dynasty (c. 1390–1295 BCE)

Tiy, queen of Amenhotep III, was never relegated to the background. A commemorative scarab issued soon after her husband's accession confirmed to the world that she that was "the king's principal wife.... The name of her father is Yuya and the name of her mother is Thuyu."[37] This unnecessary naming of the queen's parents is highly unusual and was presumably intended to stress that although she was of non-royal birth, Tiy was indeed the consort whose children would inherit the throne.

Tiy was regularly depicted alongside Amenhotep both on public monuments and in private tombs, her cartouche was linked with his on official inscriptions and personal items, and she was mentioned in diplomatic correspondence.[38] The only prominent role that she did not play was that of "God's Wife of Amun." Instead, Tiy was closely identified with the solar goddesses Hathor, Maat, and Tefnut; she became the first queen to include the cow horns and sun disk of Hathor in her crown, and she regularly carried the *sistrum*. Middle Kingdom queens had occasionally been depicted as female sphinxes who acted as passive observers in scenes involving their pharaohs. Tiy was the first to be shown actively defending her land. A tiny scene in Kheruef's tomb (TT 192) shows Tiy as a sphinx trampling two female prisoners, while the Nubian Sedeinga temple shows Tiy as a sphinx stalking across the top of the temple pillars.[39] This temple, a subsidiary to Amenhotep's neighboring Soleb temple, confirms that the royal couple, while hovering on the verge of divinity in Egypt, are to be regarded as fully divine in Nubia.

Prominent though she was, Tiy was not the only "Great Wife" at Amenhotep's court. Toward the end of his reign, Tiy's eldest daughter, Sitamen, started to use the title, although she never took precedence over her mother. The obvious implication is that Sitamen had married her father, although this is never explicitly stated.[40] Their marriage is so unusual that it leads us to ask whether it was a true marriage or simply a means of providing the aging Tiy with a young co-queen to assist in the performance of religious duties that are likely to have been, at least in part, connected with fertility and the stimulation of both the gods and the king. However, we should not inflict our own cultural values on 18th-Dynasty Egypt. There was divine precedent for father-daughter unions—Re married his daughter Hathor—and this would have formed an attractive model for a king interested in developing his own solar-based divinity.

Tiy's younger son inherited his throne as Amenhotep IV. Soon after his accession, he changed his name to Akhenaten, "Living Spirit of the Aten." Within five years Akhenaten had abolished most of the established pantheon and replaced Egypt's many deities with the ancient solar god known as the Aten. His consort, Nefertiti, changed her name too, becoming Neferneferuaten-Nefertiti ("Beautiful are the Beauties of the Aten, a Beautiful Woman has Come"). The court now moved to a new capital city, Akhetaten, or Amarna: it is from this city that the era today known as the Amarna Period takes its name.

Nefertiti was not of royal birth.[41] Her parents are never mentioned, but indirect evidence from the Amarna tomb of Ay suggests that she too was a member of the Egyptian elite, possibly Ay's own daughter. Whatever her parentage, Nefertiti was accorded great respect. Within her cartouche the writing of the name of the Aten was reversed so that it faced the determinative sign, indicating Nefertiti's status; this transposition was a great honor as it allowed the queen's image to face the name of her god. Occasionally Nefertiti's name was written in two cartouches, so that it resembled that of a pharaoh.

The many surviving images of Nefertiti allow us to see how her face and body alter in line with the evolving Amarna art style: as her husband's reign progresses she changes from a stereotypical young woman to a near mirror image of the king before returning to a more lifelike appearance.[42] Nefertiti's wigs and headdresses, too, evolve until she develops her own unique crown, a tall, straight-edged, flat-topped blue helmet-shaped headdress whose shape recalls the sprouting crown worn by Tefnut.

It is clear that Nefertiti was allocated a prominent role in the new religion.[43] In the Theban *hwt bnbn* temple she was able to perform pharaoh's role of offering to the Aten with her eldest daughter, Meritaten, acting as her assistant. Later, in scenes carved on private stelae at Amarna, she was presented to the people as an object of worship and an emblem of divine fertility. But her political importance is less obvious, and the evidence is contradictory. Unlike Tiy, she is never mentioned in diplomatic correspondence, yet she often appears at true scale beside her husband, while her title, "Lady of the Two Lands," emphasizes her role as Akhenaten's feminine counterpart. She is even depicted smiting a female enemy. This has led to various suggestions that Nefertiti may have grown powerful enough to have acted as Akhenaten's co-regent before serving either as co-regent with Tutankhamen or as sole pharaoh. However, as yet, there is no unequivocal evidence to support these theories, and it may be argued with equal validity, accepting the principle of Occam's razor, that Nefertiti died and was buried at Amarna during her husband's reign.[44]

Events immediately following Akhenaten's death are confused, but it is clear that within a couple of years the throne passed to Tutankhaten—a king of unknown parentage who, we may speculate, was the son of Akhenaten and his harem queen Kiya. Tutankhaten took as his consort Ankhesenpaaten, Nefertiti's third daughter. Soon, the newly renamed Tutankhamen and Ankhesenamen attempted to erase all memory of the Amarna Period. They abandoned Amarna, reinstated the old pantheon, and returned the court to Thebes.

Ankhesenamen continued her mother's high public profile, appearing on many of Tutankhamen's public monuments and on more private items recovered from his tomb where she takes the role of Maat to offer divine support to her husband. When Tutankhamen died, she vanished from the historical record, and we might reasonably assume that she retired to one of the harem palaces were it not for one curious incident. A copy of a contemporary cuneiform letter has been recovered from the Hittite capital, Boghaskoy:[45]

> My husband has died. I do not have a son. But, they say, you
> have many sons. If you would give me one of your sons he would

become my husband. I shall never pick out a servant of mine
and make him my husband.... He will be my husband and king
of Egypt.

The name of the letter writer is simply given as *Dahamenzu*, a phonetic version of the standard queen's title *ta hemet nesu(t)*. The Hittite king was highly
suspicious; everyone knew that Egyptian princesses did not marry outside their
own family. But the letter proved too great a temptation. A prince, Zannanza,
was sent to Egypt only to die on the Egyptian border. It may be that the letter
was not written by any Egyptian queen. But if the message is genuine, it may
well have been written by Ankhesenamen.

Ramesside Queens (Dynasties 19 and 20 c. 1295–1069 BCE)

Although this valley had been used occasionally as a burial place during the
18th Dynasty, the 19th Dynasty saw the development of *Ta set neferu*, the Valley
of the Queens or "the Place of Beauties," as a cemetery for the more important
royal wives and their children.

The first two Ramesside queens, Sitre and Tuya, were highborn ladies
who married before their husbands became heirs to the throne. In marked
contrast to the highly conspicuous royal women of Amarna, they reverted to
the traditional consort's role of offering passive support to their husbands
and sons. Tuya, however, did gain increased prominence during the reign
of her son, Ramesses II, when she featured prominently in his divine birth
legend. Ramesses II, an unusually long-lived monarch who reigned for sixty-
eight years, outlived most of his wives and, indeed, many of his children. He
therefore had several consorts. Although we know their names—Nefertari,
Iset-Nofret I, his daughters Bint-Anath I, Meritamen and Nebet-Tawi, the
ephemeral Henutmire, the Hittite-born Maat-Hor-Neferure—we can say very
little about these women. Nefertari, his longest-serving and therefore best-
known consort, is featured twice, at colossal size, on the face of the Lesser
Temple at Abu Simbel in Nubia. This is not, however, an indication that she
was considered a person of importance in her own right. Nefertiti, who carries
the *sistrum* and wears the cow horns associated with Hathor, is offering her
feminine support to the husband who is worshipped alongside the traditional
gods at the neighboring Great Temple, and to avoid any doubt about their relative importance, Ramesses himself appears four times, at colossal size, on the
facade of the Lesser Temple. Merenptah, thirteenth-born son and successor to
Ramesses II, maintained this tradition of the passive wife, as did his ultimate
successor Sety II. It is only with the final queen of the 19th Dynasty, Tausret,
that we meet a woman whom we can once again describe as an individual.

Tausret is, of course, the subject of this book and her reign is described in detail in Chapter 2.

Dynasty 20 was founded by the obscure Sethnakht, for whom Tausret's tomb was later used. Little is known about his consort Tiy-Merenese, mother of Ramesses III. Nor, indeed, is much known about Iset Ta-Hemdjert, consort of Ramesses III (Figure 1.3, see insert). Ramesses ruled at a time when Egyptian prosperity was threatened by foreign invaders and by poor harvests, which led to food shortages, inflation, and civil unrest at Thebes. Meanwhile the increasingly powerful priesthood of Amun was starting to pose a serious challenge to royal authority. Pharaoh maintained a large harem that provided him with at least ten sons. This was to be his downfall.[46]

A collection of contemporary court papers preserves the details of a plot masterminded from the "harem of the accompanying" by the otherwise unknown harem queen Tiy.[47] Ramesses was to be killed and the throne was to pass to Tiy's son who is given the false name "Pentaweret" ("The [male] One of the [female] Great One"). Two nearly identical documents, *Papyrus Rollin* and *Papyrus Lee*, give us an idea of the sequence of events:[48]

> It happened because writings were made for enchanting, for ban-
> ishing and confusing. Because some gods and some men were
> made of wax....He was examined and substance was found to every
> allegation and every crime....These were offences that merited
> death....And when he understood that the offences that he had
> committed were worthy of death, he brought death upon himself.

Ramesses was eventually attacked as he celebrated a religious festival at his Medinet Habu temple, on the west bank at Thebes. The conspirators were apprehended, however, and three separate trials saw thirty-eight people condemned to death, either by their own hands or by execution. Pentaweret was found guilty of plotting with his mother and was allowed to commit suicide. Tiy presumably suffered the same fate although we have no record of her trial. Then proceedings took an unexpected turn, as some of the judges and officials were arrested and charged with gross misconduct with the ladies of the harem. Only one judge was cleared of the charges against him.

Ramesses III was followed by eight further Ramesses. We know little about these pharaohs and even less about their consorts who are, to all intents and purposes, invisible to us. This situation continues until 305 BCE when the Ptolemies burst on the scene. However, if we can say little about Egypt's later dynastic queens, we can say something about their daughters, the "God's Wives of Amun." By the 25th Dynasty the "God's Wife" had enjoyed a major increase in status. "God's Wives" now performed temple rituals that had once been reserved for pharaoh and his deputies. They wrote their names in cartouches, and they wore the double-plumed headdress that caused them to resemble both queens and goddesses. Their role, originally a purely religious one, had become almost entirely political. Effectively the celibate "God's Wife" and her adopted successors ruled Thebes—curtailing the power of the High Priests—on behalf of their fathers, the northern kings who ruled from the Delta. This tradition of powerful, royal-born "God's Wives" would last until the Persian invasion.

Ptolemaic Queens (305–30 BCE)

Alexander the Great took Egypt from the Persians in 332 BCE. But he and his successors, Philip Arrhidaeos and Alexander IV, were remote pharaohs. To all intents and purposes Egypt lacked a queen until Ptolemy I revived the monarchy, ruling from the new city-port of Alexandria. His was a very different rule. Superficially, *maat* was maintained. Pharaohs published monumental texts in the hieroglyphic script; they fought off enemies, restored state temples, and wore traditional regalia to offer to the ancient gods. But the new pharaohs were of Macedonian heritage, and they lived and, presumably, thought as Macedonians. As Greek became the language of the court, Egypt acquired, for the first time, a word—*basilia*—that equates to our modern word "queen."

The Ptolemaic queen-consorts drew upon ancient dynastic tradition to reinforce their position and assume unprecedented divine power. As murderous feuding and repeated brother-sister marriages drastically reduced the royal family, Ptolemaic queens were called upon to rule, either alongside sons or brothers or in their own right: like Hatshepsut before her, the most famous Ptolemaic queen, Cleopatra VII, never actually ruled without a male co-ruler. Contemporary with the well-documented Classical world, we know far more about these Ptolemaic queens than we do about their predecessors; there is therefore a danger that, becoming fascinated by their stories, we might overestimate their importance while simultaneously underestimating the importance of their "invisible" dynastic predecessors. As the Ptolemaic queens ruled a thousand years after Tausret, they had no impact on her life, although she, of course, may have impacted their role. They are included in this introductory chapter, albeit briefly, because, by establishing the whole range of Egypt's female rulers, they help us to place Tausret in her true historical context.

The first influential Ptolemaic queen, Arsinoë II, was the sister-consort of Ptolemy II. Their marriage caused a scandal in the Hellenistic world, where brother-sister incest was shunned, but it linked the new royal family to the pharaohs of old, and it set a precedent that most Ptolemies would follow. Ptolemaic sisters, destined from birth to rule alongside their brothers, now assumed an increasingly prominent political and religious role. They developed their own regalia and held their own assets, barges, and bank accounts.

To deal with their new responsibilities they were educated by tutors from the Alexandrian Museion. However, while incest was back in fashion, polygamy was not. The Ptolemies practiced serial monogamy, taking one partner at a time, remarrying after death or divorce and, in many cases, maintaining mistresses whose children were not considered legitimate.

There had always been uncertainty over the exact nature of royal divinity. Ptolemy II swept away all confusion by establishing the royal cults. Now all Ptolemaic rulers joined the dynastic cult during their lifetime. This group divinity might then be supplemented by a personal divinity either at death (during the earlier part of the Ptolemaic period) or during their own lifetime (during the later part of the Ptolemaic period). In 272–271 BCE Ptolemy II and Arsinoë II together became the living "Brother-Sister Gods" (*Theoi Adelphoi*). Arsinoë II was the first Ptolemaic queen to be shown supporting pharaoh as he offered to the gods, the first to wear the double uraeus, and the only queen to develop her own crown incorporating traditional Egyptian symbolism. Her image, in both Hellenistic and traditional Egyptian style, spread throughout the Ptolemaic empire on coins, vases, statues, and reliefs, while back home her name was celebrated in the growing number of towns named Arsinoë. An early death, in c. 270 BCE, led to a posthumous deification and a personal cult based at Alexandria.

The late second century BCE saw the Ptolemies almost destroyed by inter-family strife as brother kings Ptolemy VI and Ptolemy VIII competed for the throne. This domestic discord had the effect of strengthening the role of their queens, with Ptolemy VIII in particular realizing that an association with a powerful consort would enhance his own position. As queen to her brother Ptolemy VI, Cleopatra II earned the respect of the Alexandrians and achieved a status of near equality with her brother. Subsequently, as consort to her brother Ptolemy VIII, she was challenged by her daughter Cleopatra III. Cleopatra married her stepfather Ptolemy VIII in 140 BCE. Already, before she became queen, she had a personal divinity. Following her marriage, Cleopatra became the living embodiment of Isis, becoming totally identified with the goddess in all her aspects. She was by now the most divine of the divine Ptolemaic queens. Yet, following the death of Ptolemy VIII, she felt it necessary to award herself three further cults.

In 80 BCE Ptolemy XII came to the throne almost by accident: the illegitimate son of Ptolemy IX, he inherited because more suitable heirs had either died or been killed. All his children—three daughters and two sons—would eventually rule Egypt. The eldest, Berenice IV, took advantage of her father's visit to Rome to seize his throne in 58 BCE. As an unmarried queen, she would ideally have married one of her two brothers, but as the elder was little more than three years old, she chose an insignificant cousin, Seleucos. Their marriage was not a success, and Berenice had her husband strangled within a week of the wedding. Her second husband, Archelaos, lasted longer, and the two

Isis and Osiris

Long ago, the god Osiris ruled Egypt with his sister-wife Isis as his queen (Figure 1.4, see insert). Osiris was a wise and popular monarch; while he taught men to cultivate crops, Isis taught their wives how to bake bread and brew beer. When Osiris travelled the world, Isis ruled on his behalf.[49]

But Seth, brother of Osiris and Isis, believed that he should be king. Hatching a fiendish plot, he sealed Osiris into an elaborately decorated coffin and threw it into the Nile. Osiris vanished, and Seth became pharaoh. But Isis would not accept that Osiris was lost. She sought out her husband and brought his body home. Later, when Seth hacked his brother's corpse into many pieces, she transformed into a bird to recover his remains. Using her magical powers she gave him a semblance of life. Nine months later she gave birth to his son, Horus. As Osiris retired to rule Egypt's dead, Isis protected Horus until he was old enough to rule the living Egypt. This story of Isis and Osiris explains the relationship between the living king (the Horus king) and his dead predecessor (the Osiris king), while introducing us to Isis, the model wife and queen. In good times Isis remains in the background, supporting her husband, stepping forward to rule on his behalf when he is absent and retreating again on his return. But at a time of crisis she is quite capable of independent action. She is able to use her wits and courage to protect the interests of her husband and their son.

ruled with the full support of the people of Alexandria until, in 55 BCE, Ptolemy XII retook his throne and had his daughter executed.

Ptolemy's youngest daughter, Arsinoë IV, was proclaimed queen during the Alexandrian wars of 48–47 BCE. Her brief reign came to an abrupt end after a few weeks, when Julius Caesar's allies took Alexandria. She was sent to Rome to be exhibited in a triumph, then exiled to Ephesus where she was eventually murdered on Mark Antony's orders.

Ptolemy's middle daughter, Cleopatra VII (Figure 1.5, see insert), became Egypt's last, and most famous, queen.[50] The bare bones of her story are familiar to almost everyone, if not from the writings of the Classical authors, then from Shakespeare, stage and screen, and a wide range of popular fiction. Having inherited a virtually bankrupt Egypt from her father, Cleopatra spent two decades restoring prosperity while persuading Rome not to invade her increasingly wealthy land. To do this she formed personal alliances, first with Julius Caesar, and then with Mark Antony. Defeated, with Antony, at the battle of Actium in 31 BCE, she committed suicide in Alexandria in 30 BCE. Her death marked the end of Egypt as an independent state.

Cleopatra VII never ruled alone. She was the dominant co-ruler first with her brother Ptolemy XIII, then with her brother Ptolemy XIV, then, finally, with her son Ptolemy XV Caesar (Caesarion). Family tradition suggests that she would have married Ptolemy XIII soon after their father's death, but their marriage is nowhere recorded. Nor, following the death of Ptolemy XIII in 47 BCE, is there any record of a marriage with the even younger Ptolemy XIV. The birth of her son, sometime between 47 and 44 BCE, freed her from any obligation to remain associated with her brother, and it is perhaps no coincidence that Ptolemy XIV died not long after the assassination of Julius Caesar (Caesarion's rumored father) made it clear that Caesarion's future lay in Egypt, not Rome.

Caesarion's birth was intensely important to Cleopatra. With a son by her side she could develop a new identity as a divine mother—an identity that would be instantly recognizable to both her Egyptian and her Greek subjects. Cleopatra was already a living goddess. But now she was specifically identified with the Graeco-Roman Isis. This version of Isis was a mother, a healer, and a powerful magician. She was the ideal role model for any queen, and for any single mother. In 36 BCE, Cleopatra VII became the Younger Goddess. Two years later she became the New Isis, a title that distinguished her from Cleopatra III while linking her to her father Ptolemy XII, who was known as the New Dionysos. The cult of Cleopatra-Isis proved popular throughout Egypt, and long after Cleopatra's suicide—indeed, long after the introduction of Christianity—a statue of the goddess-queen was still being worshipped on Philae Island.

Conclusion

The royal family stood at the heart of political and religious life in ancient Egypt. In the absence of any contemporary definition of their roles, this chapter has examined the social and historical forces that defined kingship and queenship before and after the reign of Tausret. Using a combination of archaeological and textual evidence, and focusing on the role of the royal woman, it has set Tausert into her proper social and historical context and provides the background necessary to a more specific study of Tausert and her reign.

2

Female Horus: The Life and Reign of Tausret

GAE CALLENDER

> While he pondered thus in mind and heart, forth then from her fragrant high-roofed chamber came Helen, like Artemis of the golden arrows; and with her came Adraste, and placed for her a chair, beautifully wrought, and Alcippe brought a rug of soft wool and Phylo a silver basket, which Alcandra had given her, the wife of Polybus, who dwelt in Thebes of Egypt, where greatest store of wealth is laid up in men's houses. He gave to Menelaus two silver baths and two tripods and ten talents of gold.
>
> Homer, the *Odyssey*, 4.120

A Homeric Aside...

Homer in his poem, the Odyssey, mentions a king named Polybus and his wife Alcandra, who lived in the Theban capital of Egypt at the time of the Trojan War. George Syncellus, a Byzantine monk who was interested in chronology, refers in his Epitome of Manetho's history (Fragment 55) to this story at the end of his list of kings for Egypt's 19th Dynasty. Syncellus says that there lived at the end of the 19th Dynasty a certain *"Thuoris, who in Homer is called Polybus, husband of Alcandra, and in whose time Troy was taken."* Syncellus adds that Thuoris/Polybus reigned for seven years—a date close to the known regnal date of Queen Tausret. Despite Manetho's reference to "Thuoris" as a male king, the name certainly reflects that of Tausret.

The period of time is said to have coincided with the Trojan War, an event which is still a subject of fierce debate, some scholars proffering various dates, others saying that the Trojan War is only a legend. Troy does exist, however, and even though there does not seem to have been a single ten-year war at Troy, there is evidence for a series of bitter battles and sieges at that place about this time. The usual date given for the ending of the legendary Trojan War is 1183 BCE, which fits in well with the regnal period of Siptah and Tausret.

Tausret lived in difficult times, and her own life was threaded with warfare and other personal troubles. She was probably born near the very end of the reign of Ramesses the Great. During the years that followed the death of this king, there was constant turmoil throughout the wider area of the East, as attested by many accounts of savage raids and sieges.[1] Great cities (such as Ugarit, Qatna, Kadesh, and Alalakh) were destroyed by hordes of armed men from varied unspecified countries. People were attacked and displaced throughout the Near East and Eastern Mediterranean and they became refugees. While Egypt did not suffer the warfare, burning, and looting of its cities that took place in Cyprus, Anatolia, Syria, and Palestine, its Near Eastern allies did; as a result, trade declined and the supplies of metals and luxury goods shriveled up before disappearing altogether, eventually bringing to an end the greatest period of Egyptian prosperity.

Egypt itself was threatened with warfare on many occasions during the decades that followed the death of Ramesses II, and this external pressure put great strain upon the monarchy. Times were not so prosperous for Egypt's citizens either, and food shortages occasionally occurred. There was trouble within the government at home, too: the fact that the reign of Ramesses lasted sixty-seven years meant that it was his thirteenth son, Merenptah, who gained the throne as an aging man, and he reigned for only twelve years. Although he was a strong ruler, his reign was fully tested.

Merenptah's earliest campaigns were responses to several disturbances that occurred in the Near East, in the region of Canaan, but the greatest danger to Egypt's security was during Year 5 and it came from the west. An army of Libyans that had been augmented by groups of piratical foreigners, such as the Ekwesh, Shekelesh, Tursha, Lukka, and Shardana,[2] streamed over the border of Libya and entered the northwestern regions of the Delta. Many of their numbers were landless men hiring themselves out as mercenary soldiers, and they had allied themselves with Libya's king, Meryre. Since this horde brought with them wives, children, livestock, and household furniture, they evidently planned on settling in the Delta—as the Hyksos groups had done from the east almost 400 years earlier. Egyptian records suggest that this combined horde of Libyans and other peoples must have been huge in numbers because records say that the dead exceeded well over 16,000 (9,300 being Libyans alone) and the captives numbered over 9,000;[3] we do not learn how many Egyptian soldiers and *their* foreign squads were killed. Despite the size of the menace, Merenptah's army was successful in defeating it, and huge numbers of prisoners were taken, some to swell the ranks of slaves and some to settle into army encampments in the Delta, where they acted as auxiliary forces whose job was to deter other invaders. Records show that there were large groups of Near Eastern peoples within the Delta towns of this period and later, some of whom listed their occupations as military men—often in charge of army divisions of different sizes.

The settlement of this campaign may have restored peace to the northern regions of Egypt for the meantime (during the reign of Ramesses III the hordes were to return), but the general climate in Egypt was very volatile: pirates continued to raid the eastern Mediterranean coastlines and, to the south, there was a rebellion in Nubia to add to Merenptah's troubles. Moreover, when Merenptah died, there was serious dissent among the members of the royal family regarding the succession, and Tausret—perhaps no more than a teenager at this time—became caught up in it.

The Reigns of Sety II and Amenmesse

Sety II had been the eldest son of Merenptah[4] and he should have succeeded his father, but for some unknown reason, Sety's reign was challenged by a man known as Amenmesse, who also carried the pharaonic title of "Ruler of Upper and Lower Egypt." We do not know this man's origins—it is assumed he was a royal prince, perhaps a son of either Ramesses or Merenptah—nor precisely when he took the throne, but he was certainly in control of the Theban area down to Nubia from Years 2–4 of Sety's reign. Sety's own reign may have been confined to the northern regions of Egypt, but the few records we have do not clarify the situation: only one record of Amenmesse has been found in northern Egypt, but Sety II has few records there either. When Amenmesse's reign came to an end, however, his names and titles were erased from his monuments and reinscribed with the name of Sety II.[5] These alterations have resulted in confusing and at times ambiguous records so that even today the historical outline is uncertain.

It is likely that reprisals took place against those who had sided with the cause of Amenmesse.[6] A couple of incidents among the workmen's community at Deir el Medina seem to indicate that even these people were affected by the larger political scene;[7] and if this is so, we can assume that retribution also occurred higher up the social ladder. Whenever Egyptian kings had very short reigns there was unrest among the population, and we get increased reports of robbery and violence—true for this time as well. A generation later, the workers in the village staged a couple of strikes, the first time this had ever occurred anywhere in world history. Thievery was frequent: during the funerary procedures for Sety II, we learn that Paneb, one of the workmen in the Valley of the Kings, was even accused of stealing some of the dead king's burial equipment.

We know very little about Sety's life or reign, but it has been said that his most important wife in his earliest years was a princess named Takhat. This woman was the mother of Amenmesse, but she was not necessarily Sety's wife. Takhat was originally entitled "King's Mother" on one statue of Amenmesse now stored in the Egyptian Museum, Cairo: that inscription was later erased— probably by agents of King Sety II—so it is possible that she may have been a wife of either Merenptah or even Ramesses II. Without doubt, Takhat was the mother of Amenmesse. However, there are several members of the royal family from Ramesses II onward who were named Takhat,[8] and sorting out these women is difficult.

It has been said that Takhat, the mother of Amenmesse, was the same person as the last owner of a sarcophagus lid that was found in the tomb of Amenmesse.[9] However, this lid owner may have been a later queen of the same name and not the mother of Amenmesse at all. Amenmesse's tomb had been stripped of his name and titles and he was declared to be "The Enemy," so it is unlikely that either his wife or his mother would have been buried in his original tomb. To my mind, there is a greater likelihood that Amenmesse's mother belonged to an earlier period than the time of Sety II[10] because if Sety came to the throne at nineteen or twenty years of age (as the mummy attributed to him suggests), he could not have fathered a son (Amenmesse) who was old enough to usurp a throne. Curiously, the fact that the six Karnak statues analyzed by Frank Yurko were all usurped plays a part in this identification issue. Although Yurko[11] has shown that one of these statues, CG 1198, was usurped by Sety II, he also admits that the original statue with its inclusion of Queen Takhat's image, name, and titles on its right-hand side could have been usurped from Merenptah; this would make good sense for Amenmesse's usurpation if, as mentioned above, he had been a member of the family of Ramesses rather than of Merenptah. Apart from her parental identity, Takhat played no further part in the story of Sety's family and we know that, at least by Year 2 of Sety II's reign, his principal wife was Queen Tausret.

Tausret's origins are not known. As she seems to have been a young woman[12] at the time that Merenptah had died, we suspect that she may have been a granddaughter of Ramesses II, for the title of "King's Daughter" is never found with inscriptions containing the queen's titles. The earliest record we have featuring Tausret's name comes from her tomb in the Valley of the Kings; the record was written in Year 2, first month of Peret (Winter), day 8 of the reign of Sety II. The fact that the queen was being given a tomb in the

Valley of the Kings is quite astonishing for, by Dynasty 19, the majority of royal wives were buried in their own valley cemetery (the Valley of the Queens) just over a kilometer to the east. There must have been an important reason for this overturning of tradition, but we are ignorant of it.

On day 19 of Winter in Year 6 of his reign, Sety died (c. 1194 BCE). If the mummy labeled CG 61037 in the Egyptian Museum, Cairo, is his, it shows that he was still a youngish man when he died; his cause of death is as yet unknown. Grafton Elliot Smith[13] was able to observe at the examination of this mummy that he was a "young or middle-aged man" with "closely-clipped, dark brown hair." Like many others, this mummy had been stripped of its valuables and its coffin, but it did have his name written on the linen wrapped around his emaciated body. To date, the identification of this mummy has not been seriously challenged, so if it does belong to Sety II, the forensic X-ray charts give him an age of twenty-five.[14] This youthful date is confirmed by the fact that his bones show no lipping at all, indicating that he must have been quite young when he died. Because of the youth of the mummy, we can assume that his probable wife, Tausret, would also have been in her twenties—or possibly younger—when her husband died. Needless to say, if the mummy is not that of Sety, then these calculations are invalid.

The Reign of Siptah and Regency of Tausret

Sety II was succeeded by Ramesses-Siptah, whose mother was a *ḥmt nswt* (or "King's Wife"), Šoteraja, a Canaanite woman. The name of Siptah's father is never stated on the artifacts known to us at present, but the young king changed his name from Ramesses-Siptah to Merenptah-Siptah, possibly suggesting that Siptah was a direct descendant of Merenptah—perhaps either a son or grandson. As his mother was a Canaanite, it is possible that Šoteraja came to Egypt as a result of those Canaanite campaigns conducted by Merenptah earlier on in his reign.

In later times, the name of Siptah was omitted from various types of official records: it was as if he had never existed. Siptah is usually referred to as a son of Sety, but such a hostile attitude would have been inexplicable if Sety had been Siptah's father, because Sety II remained an admired ruler to later Egyptian officials.[15] Tutankhamen was omitted from later records because there had been a *damnatio* deleting the memory of his father, Akhenaten, but there seems to be no reason for a son of either Merenptah or Sety II to have been treated like this. The *damnatio* for Siptah thus permits the possibility that he might have been Amenmesse's son, because Amenmesse was indeed considered an "Enemy" and his records were either damaged or his name was removed from public records. Cyril Aldred certainly thought that Amenmesse had been the father of Siptah.[16] Leonard Lesko,[17] however, points out that Siptah usurped two stelae of

Amenmesse, which is hardly the proper act of a son. We might also entertain the idea that Siptah changed his name from Ramesses-Siptah to Merenptah-Siptah because Amenmesse was a son of Ramesses II and he wished to dissociate himself from the same hereditary link as "the Enemy"—as Amenmesse was called.

Thus, Sety II and Amenmesse both have arguments against their possible parentage. Siptah's apparent age at death would allow for any one of the kings Merenptah, Amenmesse, or Sety II to have been his father, but the coincidence of his mother being a Canaanite woman does rather favor Merenptah as a father. Perhaps the antipathy toward Siptah—he is even omitted from Manetho's list of Egyptian kings composed during the Ptolemaic era—was just a consequence of hostility toward Asiatics, due to the Asiatic invasions of that era and the alliance with Irsu that preceded King Sethnakht's reign (for which, see the latter part of this chapter).

The mummy that is named as Siptah is that of a lanky teenager (1.6 m in height) of about sixteen years of age. He had curly, reddish-brown hair and a rather narrow, aquiline nose. His left foot was deformed, and he may have suffered from poliomyelitis.[18] If the identification of the mummy is correct, the king must have been a young child in Merenptah's time and about ten years of age when King Sety II died.

Perhaps because of his parents,[19] and certainly because of the youthful age at which he came to the throne, Siptah was put in the charge of a regent who, as usual, was the chief wife of the most recently deceased king. This was Tausret ("The Powerful One"—an alternative name for the cobra goddess, Wadjet). Her main title during the period of her regency (apart from her usual title of "Great Wife of the King") was *t3 rp^{c}t ^{c}3t n t3 nb*—usually rendered as "Great Regent of all the Land."[20] In his comments on the second phase of the decoration of the queen's tomb (conventionally referred to as KV 14),[21] H. Altenmüller[22] mentions a painted scene, where the queen makes an offering to Anubis and is labeled "the mistress of the Two Lands…mistress of the crowns Tausret, [beneficial to] Mut." Altenmüller is surely correct in seeing these names and titles as a reference to Tausret as regent.

In connection with her regency, J. von Beckerath[23] believes that the remains of a pair statue with the name of Siptah from this regency period show the young king Siptah as a crowned king, seated across the lap of Tausret, who sits on a box throne. There is nothing left of the larger figure, which has been hacked to pieces, but the figure of the child-king is unmistakable and his name has been found on it. Although the identification of Tausret's image has been challenged,[24] it is not part of Egyptian iconography to have a crowned king seated on the knees of a male; this is an iconic regency statue, such as we see with Queen Ankhnesmeryre II and the child-king Pepy II (Brooklyn, B 39.119).

Tausret herself seems to have had no living offspring, but it is possible that a son of Sety II—the only one present in reliefs today—might have been her child. Images of this prince still exist in a very dilapidated state in the entrance

Tausret's Titles as a Queen

R-pꜤtt, wrt ḥswt, nbt bnrt mrwt, ḥnwt SmꜤw Mḥt, ḥmt nswt wrt nbt tꜣwy
"Hereditary Princess, Great of praises, Lady Sweet of love, Mistress of Upper and Lower Egypt, King's Great Wife, Lady of the Two Lands"—these damaged titles come from the entrance to KV 14 (Altenmüller, *SAK* 10 [1983], 21 and Abb. 9). The queen also held the title of *ḥmt nṯr*—"God's Wife" [of Amun].

area of the Barque Shrine of Sety II, just inside the first pylon of Karnak Temple.[25] We do not know what happened to this young boy—it is likely that he died before Sety himself. It is also possible that the couple might have had another child who was buried in KV 56 ("the Gold Tomb") in the Valley of the Kings.[26] It is from this tomb that so much treasure associated with Queen Tausret and her husband has come (Figure 2.1). This was a child's burial, as suggested by the size of the silver gloves and the numerous rings from the hoard, but whether the child had been male or female could never be established because flood water had completely washed away the bodily remains.[27] It

FIGURE 2.1 Queen Tausret and King Sety II in a cup-pouring scene from one of the armbands found in KV 56, the Gold Tomb. The same type of scene is attested for King Akhenaten and Nefertiti and King Tutankhamen and Ankhesenamen. Drawing by Jolana Malátková.

is also possible that KV 56 had been the tomb of the prince mentioned earlier. In either case, the child would have been extremely young, as Tausret and her husband seem to have been only young adults themselves during Sety's six-year reign.

It is evident that Siptah must have been the only possible candidate for the throne after King Sety II died because, after Siptah's own death, no other Egyptian prince replaced him. As it was, his youth—and perhaps that clubbed foot of his—could have been seen as a disadvantage in a ruler for troubled times. Another disadvantage could have been his mother's foreign origins.[28] We get a hint of some reluctance on the part of the Egyptian officials to accept this young child, for his accession to the throne apparently had to be assisted by Egypt's chancellor, a man called Bay.

The Great Chancellor of Egypt, Bay

Bay is an intriguing person. At one stage he referred to himself as *ḳr n pȝ tȝ mḥy*,[29] "a foreigner from that northern land"—a statement that probably means that he came from one of the Near Eastern countries. However, this is an ambiguous remark and it can also mean "a visitor from the northern land," the land concerned being *Mḥw,* the Delta region of Lower Egypt;[30] he was evidently not from Thebes. His direct correspondence with the ruler of Ugarit is also an unusual sort of record to find at Ugarit, and it may be that his origins had made him useful in the diplomatic service of Egypt.

During the time of King Sety II, Bay had been the king's scribe and butler (he was entitled *sš nswt* and *wdpw nswt*), posts that were frequently held by Syrians at this time. But during Siptah's reign, Bay no longer mentions those titles and is recorded instead with the highly prestigious title of Chancellor of Egypt. It marks a sudden elevation in status and power, but the reason for this is unknown. Later inscriptions from Siptah's reign entitle Bay as "Sole Companion, Great Chancellor of the Entire Land" (*imy-r ḥtmty n tȝ r ḏr.f*).[31] This last title has a similar construction to Tausret's title as regent, and it was the first time that such a title had been recorded for a treasurer.

Further titles of Bay were found in most surprising circumstances, in one of the texts from the Urtenu archive (text RS 86.230), a set of correspondence tablets from the city of Ugarit, written in the time of Ammurapi, the last king of Ugarit.[32] It was composed during a time when Ugarit was being raided by pirates, who caused great devastation to the sea coast and countryside of that Mediterranean city. Bay is named as having sent a letter to the Ugaritic king at this time. In the letter, his name is written Beya, and he is entitled the "Chief of the troops of the Great King of the land of Egypt." That title is not otherwise attested for Bay, but we have very few references to this important person who, later on, was clearly punished and had his memory reviled. This military title is not inconsistent with Bay's elevated status at the time, and there is no other known person fulfilling such a post in other records from this period. In addition, the name of *Bay* was at that time very uncommon in ancient Egypt.

Most of that Ugaritic letter is destroyed, so we do not know what it was about, but the Beya of the letter is surely the only person at the beginning of the twelfth century BCE who would be dictating letters to the Ugaritic king on behalf of the Egyptian king. This damaged tablet provides us with just a glimpse of diplomatic correspondence carried out under King Siptah, and we wonder what other correspondence had taken place at that time. If Itmar Singer[33] is right about the identity of Beya, then the letter also provides a very precise date for the end of Ugarit, too: c.1193 BCE, according to him.

Most unusual in Bay's set of records are his reliefs. There are several images of the chancellor that portray him with the same size as the king and queen (see Figure 2.2 and refer to the gateway of the Amada temple in Nubia, where Siptah, Tausret, and Bay are all depicted having the same size—perhaps the first time that a commoner had been depicted like this in Egyptian art: see the reference to this monument in Chapter 3). This was—up until that time—an extraordinary occurrence. Even more astounding are the texts that accompany these illustrations. In one relief carved on a stele at Aswan (*LD* III, 202c) Bay is described as "casting out lies and presenting truth." This statement was an

FIGURE 2.2 Chancellor Bay and Siptah from a stela discovered at Aswan (after Lepsius, *Denkmäller* III 202c). Drawing by Jolana Malátková.

epithet of kings, not of royal officials, and one wonders what its real implication was. Was there some person or persons who presented some obstacle to the reign of the young Siptah? Apart from this epithet, Bay displays above his figure the title of "Great Chancellor of the Entire Land." The post of chancellor (or treasurer) was an old and prestigious office, but Bay's title was prefaced by the adjective "great," and this was extraordinary. Bay also presents himself to the reader on two occasions as one "who established the king upon the seat of his father" (LD 202c). Before this time, the epithet was one used only by gods[34] and pharaohs, and Bay's use of this and the previous royal epithet must have astounded his contemporaries. With his presence shown behind the king in the accompanying illustration, Bay is portraying himself as the protector of the king. But to what extent was he the "king-maker" that many historians[35] have said he was?

It is stated in the Aswan text referring to Bay that he assisted Siptah in attaining the throne.[36] If Siptah had been the legitimate heir to Sety II, Bay's help would assuredly not have been needed. But the father of Siptah is unknown, and there is a strong possibility that he was either Merenptah or Amenmesse. There may have been other reasons the young child needed additional help. If that is so, one needs to ask: *Why was Bay the man who established the king upon the seat of his father?* He was not the vizier, but the man in control of the treasury. In the records available to us, Bay seems to have been a loner: his power base is unknown and he does not carry the usual titles of the Egyptian nobility. Our only clue about his origins comes from the one statement he made about being a man from the North. Rather than such a solitary official providing support for the young king, one would have expected the vizier and his aides to have been prominent. What role, for example, did the High Priest of Amun, Bakenkhonsu, play at this time? He was the son of Roy, the previous High Priest—and a very powerful High Priest at that! On his Karnak statue Roy claims that the king himself (probably Merenptah) established the priesthood for him and his successors as a hereditary office. By awarding a hereditary post, the king could look to a committed support group,[37] but there is no evidence of that group in the records thus far available to us.

It has been suggested[38] that the basis of Bay's power (and the reason he points out that he was a non-Theban) may have been that he was the brother—or a close relation—of the Syrian queen who was Siptah's mother. If there had been such a relationship, it could explain his acceleration to power and, as the boy's uncle, he would have had a convincing rationale for his efforts to put Siptah on the throne. Such a relationship would also explain why the officials who cut inscriptions for Siptah made Bay's images so dominant on the royal monuments. This seems an attractive rationale, but it is, unfortunately, hypothetical. It is very unlikely that we could ever prove such a relationship between Siptah and Bay.

But it is the architectural legacy of Bay that offers the greatest surprise: Bay was the owner of a rock-cut tomb in the Valley of the Kings (KV 13) and his tomb is grouped with those of Sety II (KV 15), Siptah (KV 12), and Tausret. H. Altenmüller,[39] who excavated it, has demonstrated that Bay's tomb, far from being the usual sort for an official, was very similar to the royal tombs of the pharaohs Siptah and Tausret—indeed, his tomb possessed the same dimensions as Tausret's KV 14.[40] The second architectural legacy was the presence of Bay's name within the temple of King Siptah: each of the foundation deposits had a sandstone block with the titles and name of Bay, together with a total collection of over 100 other objects belonging to the chancellor.[41] This assumption of royal privileges and the placement, size, and royal design of his tomb have caused scholars to assume that the reign of Siptah was actually a *troika*, consisting of Siptah, Bay, and Tausret.[42] This theory has had a lasting influence over the historical interpretations in the last quarter of the twentieth century, but these interpretations must now be modified because of new and important evidence.

It has only recently been discovered that after Bay had reached the pinnacles of power and prestige for any ancient Egyptian official, he came to what the British call "a sticky end." Pierre Grandet, pursuing his work on the ostraka in the French Institute in Cairo, discovered that two of his ostraka fragments belonged together. When the pieces were joined, Grandet read a text that was quite astounding: it was a message from the Scribe of the Tomb, Paser, to the Deir el Medina workers:

1. *ḥȝ.t-sp 5 ȝbd 3 šmw, sw 27. hrw [p]n [jj-t]*
2. *jr(w)-n sš Pȝ-sr n[y] pȝ ḫ[r]j r-ḏd:*
3. *smȝ prʿȝ ʿ.w.s ḫrw ʿȝ Bʿy.*[43]

Year 5, third month of Shemu, day 27: This day, the scribe of the Tomb, Paser, has come to announce: "Pharaoh, Life! Prosperity and Health! has killed the great enemy, Bay."[44]

In one small text, decades of research and speculation were dissolved as the true ending to one of the most ambitious and interesting of officials was revealed.

This revelation sent shock waves through the Egyptological world at the time that it was published, but the original announcement must have exploded like a bomb among the workers and officials of the Egyptian population who lived in the Theban region in the twelfth century before our era. The pharaoh had executed the man who claimed to have put him on the throne, a man who had made himself the most important of all the royal officials serving Siptah. While a political assassination is not uncommon in our own national histories, nothing like this had ever been found before in Egyptian historical records. Work on Bay's incomplete tomb in the Valley of the Kings was halted and his tomb inscriptions were eventually erased. Strangely, though, those very prominent public reliefs featuring the chancellor, described earlier, were *not* destroyed, and we might well wonder why.

Bay died in the third month of summer, in the fifth year of Siptah's reign. The king died soon after, sometime around the second month of *ȝḫt*/Inundation, in Year 6;[45] he was buried in KV 47. Although there is a modest collection of records from the reign of Siptah, most of them—apart from the very interesting records relating to Chancellor Bay—are fairly unimportant. There are graffiti from Buhen, several from Wadi Halfa, Abu Simbel, Seheil, and Aswan mentioning the arrival of the king's officials on various missions, the most important being the collection of tribute from the Nubians.[46] Apparently, after Siptah's death, there were no other male descendants of Ramesses II remaining, so Tausret then assumed the titles of an Egyptian monarch.

Tausret as Pharaoh

The Regal Names of Tausret as Pharaoh

Horus: *Kȝ nḫt mry Mȝ*ᶜ*t, nb* ᶜ*n m nswt mi Tm,* "Strong Bull: Beloved of Maat, the Lord beautiful of appearance, the ruler like Atum." More commonly, Tausret was referred to as *Kȝ nḫt mry Mȝ*ᶜ*t,* "Strong Bull, beloved of Maat." Both versions take the masculine form and they are derived from the "Strong Bull" names of Ramesses II and Thutmose I. Tausret's husband's Bull name was *mry R*ᶜ, "Beloved of Re," but on two occasions Sety II substituted the name *mry Mȝ*ᶜ*t,* "Beloved of Maat."[47] In the variation between the masculine and feminine forms of her name, Tausret was following the pattern set by the female pharaohs Sobekneferu and Hatshepsut.

Nebty: *grgt Kmt w*ᶜ*f ḫȝswt,* "Founding Egypt and crushing the foreigners."[48] There is a marked similarity to the corresponding name of Ramesses II.[49] Tausret is the only ruler to have this name, perhaps reflecting foreign invasions into Egypt, or perhaps some border conflict with people from the Near East. Despite the fact that so many captives had been taken and so many Asiatics were engaged in work—either voluntary or involuntary—at the time, these people were not well regarded. The term "Asiatic" was quite often used in a derogatory fashion and, as the Elephantine Stele of Sethnakht later reported, Asiatics were blamed for disorder in Egypt at the commencement of Dynasty 20. Also significant is the similarity between Tausret's Nebty name and the third choice of Sety II's Nebty name of *mk Kmt w*ᶜ*f ḫȝswt* (CG 1198), so once again, Tausret was acknowledging her deceased husband by her choice of name.

Son of Re (Birth name): *Tȝ-Wsrt,* "Tausret"—"the Wosret/the female powerful/fiery One"—was often supplemented by *stp n Mwt* "chosen of Mut" within the cartouche.[50] (Note the choice of a goddess, rather than a god, again hinting at Tausret's gender.) Sometimes this title is written as *Son of Re,* at other times it is *Daughter of Re.* (The back pillar and the left-hand column of the Heliopolis statue have the *sȝ R*ᶜ masculine title, while other epithets on this sculpture are feminine.)[51] J. von Beckerath[52] provides six variations of this name. Some of its forms are accompanied by "Beloved (male) of Hathor, Mistress of the Red Mountain (i.e.,. Kom el Ahmar)."

King of Upper and Lower Egypt (*nswt bity*, **or Throne name**): *s3t R^c mry 'Imn*, "Daughter of Re, beloved of Amun;" or, with the typical title of the wife of a king: *ḥnwt t3 mḥy*, "Mistress of Lower Egypt." Von Beckerath[53] again provides six variations of this name. Among other records, this is found as part of the name for Tausret's temple.

Golden Horus: no doubt she had such a name, but this is not in our records, though there is a gold sign (without the falcon) following each cartouche on the right-hand side of her Heliopolis statue. Perhaps the addition of this sign may have been either her Golden Horus name, or part of her Horus name.[54]

In common with other pharaohs, Tausret has the title of "Lord of Appearances," but she also used the titles of "Lady of the Two Lands" as well as the masculine "Lord of the Two Lands," thus continuing the vacillation between male and female titles which is found in the titulary of other female pharaohs. Tausret's separate titles are scattered across her various monuments, but the largest collection of them—the four names and titles mentioned in this section—are engraved on an exquisite sandstone statue (see Figure 2.3) from the Heliopolis region.[55] Although the head is missing, the statue is in fine condition.

For some of these names, the epithet, "beloved of Hathor, Lady of the Red Mountain" is added: this was most likely because the sandstone came from the area of the Red Mountain (*Kom Ahmar*), which is on the outskirts of Cairo today. The statue is identical in style to the famous black granite statue of Ramesses II in Turin and is just a little smaller than life size.[56] It seems very likely that the similarity of the two statues was a deliberate attempt by the queen to associate her reign with that of Ramesses—who, it may be remembered, was probably her grandfather.

On this statue, as in all her depictions that have survived, the queen wears the beautiful flowing and pleated costume of the 19th-Dynasty depictions. To date, there are no known statues of this queen wearing the male kilt, but it should be noted that kings and queens were frequently shown wearing similar clothing from the time of Akhenaten and Nefertiti onward—that is why Tausret's dress in the statue is identical to the clothing worn by Ramesses in his Turin statue—see the bracelet illustration in Figure 2.1. She clasps the scepter in the same way that Ramesses does but, like Queen Sobekneferu and unlike most of Hatshepsut's statues,[57] her figure is feminine.

The Major Monuments of Tausret

Unlike any other queen of the Ramesside period,[58] there was no tomb for Tausret in the Valley of the Queens, even though during Sety's time she was

FIGURE 2.3 Proper left-side view of the Statue of Tausret from Medinet Nasr. Drawing by Scott Murphy after pl.VI in H. S. K. Bakry, "The Discovery of a Statue of Queen Twosre (1202–1194? B.C.) at Medinet Nasr, Cairo."

the *ḥmt nswt wrt* ("King's Great Wife"). Instead, Tausret's tomb[59] was excavated in the Valley of the Kings, a most unusual occurrence. The tomb was commenced for her in the time of Sety II and it was finished in a number of stages (see Chapter 4).

Work on her tomb was stopped during the time of Amenmesse and was recommenced in Year 2 of Siptah. Queen Tausret at this time was a regent and no doubt gave those instructions for the work to proceed once more.[60] In the same year, the first sarcophagus for Tausret was commenced (see 4.7A and 4.7B). It was hewn from granite. That sarcophagus was later removed from KV 14 and a royal sarcophagus was made: Hartwig Altenmüller thinks it may be the huge additional sarcophagus also found in Bay's tomb (see the concluding remarks in his chapter). The queenly sarcophagus must have been taken to Bay's tomb (KV 13), where its lid was uncovered by Altenmüller during his excavation of KV 13 in 1987.[61]

The tomb was completed during the remainder of her reign—although it was later altered by Ramesses III for the burial of his father, King Sethnakht. Nevertheless, the decoration of this tomb makes it one of the most beautiful monuments in the Valley of the Kings. Even as its building stages have been analyzed, so has its decoration. Numerous alterations to the original decoration were made in antiquity, many of them by Tausret herself. Siptah's images have been removed, most of Tausret's images were altered in some way for those of Sethnakht, and the cartouches were altered—in some cases, several times (Figure 2.4). The intense archaeological investigation conducted by Hartwig Altenmüller[62] over recent years has not only helped us to understand the tomb's structure, its construction stages, and the changes made to its reliefs,[63] but has also provided clues to events that took place during the reigns of the three rulers (see his chapter for details).

The tomb might be considered Tausret's most important and completed work, but there is some evidence regarding other buildings, too. For example,

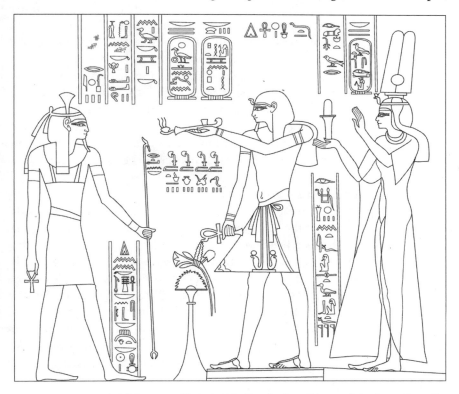

FIGURE 2.4 Portrait of Tausret, offering with Siptah, from her tomb in the Valley of the Kings. Drawing by Jolana Malátková.

one of her monuments at Giza is represented by just a single limestone block. It contains the remains of her name that came from a building whose purpose is unknown, but there is a *htp di nswt* (offering formula) involving the Memphite temple of Ptah-South-of-his-Wall and the royal *ka* of the female pharaoh,[64] so presumably it was a funerary memorial of some sort for the queen. The temple of Ptah that is mentioned had been a distribution center for the regular offerings that were made at the tombs and shrines of rulers past and present since at least the 5th Dynasty.[65]

Yet another single block with her cartouche was found in a Delta *saqqiyya* (a type of machine used to pump water from the canals) in the region of Ezbet Ziz in the Tell ed Dab`a region.[66] Like the buildings of Sety II and Siptah, it is likely to have been a small addition to an already established monument rather than a large edifice—we see a similar sort of monument in the following item recording Tausret's name.

Not far from that *saqqiyya,* at the site of Qantir, in the ancient town of Pi-Ramesses where Ramesses II had spent most of his domestic life, two large, limestone fragments from the remains of a gateway erected by King Sety II were discovered.[67] The gateway was typical of the smaller sort of monument Sety II built during his time as king. However, this is a rare record that mentions Queen Tausret as the "Great Royal Wife" in Sety II's lifetime. The fragments show part of a relief of the queen standing behind the king. The remnants of the king and queen were identified by their titles engraved just above their heads, but only two small sections of the original relief remain and the pieces do not join. The smaller piece contains the cartouches of Sety II. The larger block contains the remains of an inscription referring to Queen Tausret, and there is also part of an engraved image of the queen, who was depicted wearing a queenly crown surmounted by the *šwty*-feather decoration. No image of the king is present, just his cartouches and part of a royal formula.[68]

Another monument set up by Tausret as ruler is mentioned in the badly damaged Bilgai Stele,[69] found some 14 kms east of Sebennytos, in the Delta. That inscription records the inauguration of an *ipt*[70] for Amun in the Delta. This was a chapel that had been erected by Tausret for Amun-of-Usermaatre-Setepenre (Ramesses II), a form of Amun linked with the deified Ramesses II. The work had been carried out by an Overseer of the Fortress of the Sea whose name was erased when this stele was used as a millstone. The text of the stele is very damaged but lists the huge numbers of tribute offerings the overseer collected for that temple.[71] The chapel itself has not been identified and probably never will be because stone is a rare commodity in the damp fields of the Delta and buildings were readily dismantled so their stone blocks could be reused elsewhere.

The most substantial building project undertaken by Tausret must have been her temple, which lay in the plain in front of Hatshepsut's temple at

Deir el-Bahri. Today, however, nearly all of its masonry has been removed. Although Flinders Petrie found evidence of the building's size and a number of foundation deposits at the site, Tausret's temple was only discernible to the archaeologist because of its foundations: nothing else appeared to have remained, as far as he was concerned.[72] Fortunately, these remains have now been reexcavated by a team from the University of Arizona and they have cast new light on the hurried and only partial excavation once carried out by Petrie (see the chapter by Richard Wilkinson in this volume).

Three deposits of precious metal items from the era of Tausret are also known: these are discussed by Catharine Roehrig in her chapter of this volume. The first two hoards of gold and silver serving vessels from Bubastis (modern Tell Basta, in the Delta) include a small number of vessels bearing the names of Sety II and Tausret. Notably, some of the items are typical of Syrian workmanship,[73] suggesting that although the Near East was experiencing considerable unrest at the time, trade and commercial contacts were still being made between Egypt and the Near East. Some of Tausret's names are found on one or two objects with the double cartouches of a ruler, indicating that, at the earliest, it was in her reign that these hoards were deposited.

A jar fragment with the queen's name found in Succoth, a site in Wadi Tumilat in the northeastern Delta near the border with Palestine, and another example of her cartouches on a jar from Sidon[74] further acknowledge her contact with the Near East; it seems evident from these fragments that either occasional gift exchange or trade of some sort was taking place during her reign. Another, quite curious object containing her name is a large scarab with the cartouches of Tausret, Thutmose III, and Senusert III[75] (see Figure 2.5). It would appear to be a scarab issued by Tausret that paid homage to the famous warrior pharaohs, Thutmose III and Senusert III; however, its inscription is atypical of scarabs made at this time, and the way in which its inscription nominates the earlier kings is quite different from other commemorative scarabs. It is an interesting piece, but it is likely to be a forgery.

The third set of precious items was found by Ayrton in the flooded remains of KV 56. This is more likely to have been associated with the burial of a child and so was not a buried hoard. However, the hoarding of treasures occurs throughout history, most frequently when invasion or civil wars occur, and this fact seems to mesh well with the suggestion that the end of Tausret's reign could have been a time of conflict. Thus we can see that even though her monuments have undergone severe destruction, the pharaoh Tausret endeavored to perform the tasks of a traditional Ramesside ruler: she built monuments dedicated to the gods, conducted diplomatic exchanges with rulers to the north and east, and participated in religious affairs to the south. She may not have sought to become a ruler from the outset—perhaps the early death of her husband pushed her prominently into this role—but her guiding lights seem to have been those of Sety II and Rameses II and her royal names at least bear

(a)   (b)

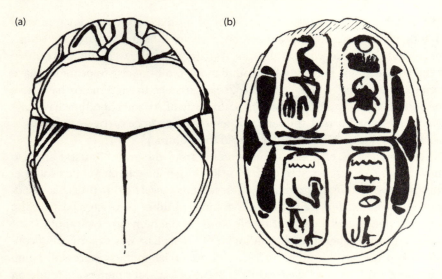

FIGURE 2.5 Scarab (a) upper surface (b) base with inscription containing the name of Tausret. Drawing by the author.

witness to this idea. We have very little information about her personal history and none at all about her personality or character; but if she did participate in warfare on behalf of her country, as an anonymous ostrokon could suggest (see Figure 2.6 and discussion), she would have been a very courageous woman. I also like to think that it was she who might have been responsible for bringing Bay's era of power to an end—again, an act of courage, especially for a woman whose own power base seems to have been rather insubstantial at the time.

Reconstructing the History of Tausret's Reign

What little information we do have about the reign of Queen Tausret mainly concerns her monuments—a similar set of circumstances also is found relating to the reigns of Amenmesse, Sety II, and Siptah. The fact that only Sety II was held in esteem by later archivists is probably the main reason for these historical blanks, but the volatility of the times and the short tenure of each of those reigns are factors that contribute to our incomplete knowledge.

Tausret reigned for well over eight years—perhaps ten or even eleven, as the new evidence from the University of Arizona excavations suggests. The female pharaoh did not date her reign from the time following the death of Siptah but, instead, included the length of his reign within her total. This was, of course, what Hatshepsut had done before her, but it was not what Sobekneferu had done. Images of her husband, Sety II, within her own tomb (KV 14) also strengthened the link she had to Sety[76] (see Chapter 4), which may have been the basis for her final transition to full rulership.

Of course, as regent, Tausret probably *had* been in charge of the major decisions made in Siptah's reign, but it is also likely that Tausret presented herself to the people as the regent of Siptah who had legitimately become the sole ruler after Sety's death.[77] Furthermore, it is not impossible that Tausret may have absorbed the reign of Siptah (as Horemheb had done with the Amarna pharaohs) in a piece of propaganda that linked her reign with that of her husband, Sety II. We know that Siptah was "forgotten" in the later records, so perhaps Tausret was endeavoring to align herself with the forces that had disapproved of Siptah's reign in the first place. Such an attitude also seems to have been the motive for the alterations made to the cartouches of Siptah in Tausret's tomb, where the cartouches of Sety II were recarved over those of Siptah. Such a precedent had already been set by Hatshepsut—although that queen had chosen to link herself to her father and actually brought his body into her own tomb.

There is an important stele from the island of Elephantine[78] (opposite Aswan) which was written at the beginning of the 20th Dynasty. It is known as the Elephantine Stele and its main theme is that at the end of the 19th Dynasty, a Syrian called *Irsu* (a name that means "he made himself") seized control in Egypt with the help of other foreigners from the Near East (they are called "Asiatics" in the text). The stele reports that the land of Egypt was in chaos and that an Egyptian hero named Sethnakht defeated this coalition of Asiatics and restored peace to Egypt once more. It is well known, of course, that Sethnakht was the founder of the 20th Dynasty. The stele does not mention Siptah, Bay, or Tausret. Previous accounts of history concerning the end of the 19th Dynasty assumed that the Syrian called Irsu was actually Chancellor Bay, and that he had removed Siptah and Tausret and seized the Egyptian throne for himself. We are now in a position to know that this historical reconstruction is inaccurate.

Although most textbooks[79] say that Tausret, Bay, and Siptah were united in helping each other to stay in power, in fact, it is now evident that there must have been considerable tension among these three people. Evidence for that was found by Pierre Grandet, when he joined two ostraka fragments (O.Ifao 1864) together and discovered that Bay not only died in Year 5 of Siptah, but also orders from the king reveal that Bay was disgraced and executed. We neither know the cause of nor the events prior to the execution, but it is more than likely that the regent Tausret would have been the prime mover against Bay. Siptah died in the following year, and Tausret became pharaoh and continued to rule beyond Year 8. After this time our sources are blank.

The closing events of the 19th Dynasty are not known, but two very important texts provide one version of what happened after the (presumed) death of Queen Tausret. The first of these texts is the Great Harris Papyrus I[80] (so-called because it is over 41 meters in length). It was written by a group of scribes during the reign of Ramesses IV, and the final section gives us a general glimpse of the times as they saw them. It ends with the death of Ramesses III and the accession of his son Ramesses IV (1153 BCE). It is not, however, to be accepted as a precise record of the actual events. The other text,[81] mentioned above, was written on a stele that was found at Elephantine. The initial passages celebrate the ending of conflict and the triumph of King Sethnakht, first king of the 20th Dynasty. (Together with R. Drenkhahn,[82] I take the date of Year 2 to be the year of the final conquest.) The second half of this text recounts incidents from the battles. This section is clearly idealized, glorifying the king rather than presenting a more trustworthy historical narrative. Nonetheless, it does contain many important pointers to the history of the reign. Both texts say that there had been chaos in the land, invasion by Asiatics; and Pap. Harris identifies one Asiatic as Irsu, who had seized control, while the Elephantine Stele refers to him obliquely as "this Asiatic" (line 11), so there does appear to have been a foreign leader asserting his presence in the land prior to Sethnakht's arrival on the scene.

Piecing together the few relevant statements and considering the few examples of archaeological evidence that have been found, it seems that Egypt was invaded in its Delta regions at least by people from the Near East. Either an Asiatic from within the population of Egypt at the time or an Asiatic leader coming in with the invaders took control in Egypt's northern regions. How far this control extended is not known. If Tausret had been alive at this time it would be expected that she would have sent out the army to drive back the invaders. Conjecturally, but given the evidence of Egyptian queens as military leaders (Ahhotep II and Hatshepsut at least), it is possible that Tausret could have accompanied the army into battle. An ostrakon[83] held in the Egyptian Museum, Cairo, gives us encouragement to think that at this stage in the history of the 19th Dynasty, Tausret might have been seen as a military leader (Figure 2.6).

Both contemporary texts mentioned earlier report that there had been great disorder in Egypt, followed by "empty years"—kingless years—when a Syrian named Irsu was in power, but lawlessness reigned and the temples were neglected. All this was prior to the emergence of Sethnakht from Egypt's south. Here is what our two records have to say:

Papyrus Harris I. Sections 398 and 399:

> The land of Egypt was in a state of flux, every man being a law unto himself, and they had had no leader for many years previously, until the time came when the land of Egypt consisted of princes and mayors, one man killing his fellow among high and low. Then another time came after it, consisting of empty years, when Irsu the Asiatic was with them as chief, and he made the entire land subservient before him. Each joined with his neighbor in plundering their goods, and they treated the gods as they did men, so that none dedicated

FIGURE 2.6 An Egyptian queen, mounted on a war chariot, fires arrows at a male opponent on a 20th-Dynasty ostrakon in the Egyptian Museum, Cairo (CG 25125) discovered in KV 9 in the Valley of the Kings. Drawing by Jolana Malátková.

offerings in their holy places. But the gods turned themselves to peace so as to put the land in its proper state in accordance with its normal conditions, and they established their son who came forth from their flesh as ruler of every land upon their great throne, even User-khaure-setpenre-meryamun, the Son of Re Sethnakht-meryre-Amun.[84]

Elephantine stele, lines 4, 7-11:

" . . . this land was in disorder. Egypt had fallen into a state of neglect of the gods . . . " His Majesty Life! Flourishing! Health! [Sethnakht] is like his father, Seth, who stretches out both his arms around Egypt, to purify it through this expulsion of him who attacks, as his strength is around about it [Egypt] as a protection. His adversary falls before him, as he has put fear into their hearts. They flee back [as small birds], when the falcon is behind them. They leave behind their possessions of silver, gold and copper in Egypt, that they intended to give this Asiatic. . . .

The similarity of the texts is obvious—as was pointed out by Rosemarie Drenkhahn[85] many years ago. Most striking is the report in both accounts of treasure being extorted by the Asiatics—the vivid scene of those people dropping their stolen treasure as they fled from the victorious Egyptians—*Pap. Harris I* being particularly memorable. Drenkhahn[86] has suggested that the Elephantine stele and Papyrus Harris accounts might offer a new interpretation for the burial of the two Bubastis hoards and she could be right.

There are other considerations too. All the suggestions that Irsu was Chancellor Bay must now be abandoned: Bay had died long before even Tausret took the throne. But the question is, who was the Syrian Irsu who played such a prominent political role prior to Sethnakht's accession to the Egyptian throne? Victors write the history of their period and we should be cautious about accepting their accounts, so we must ask ourselves: was King Sethnakht reporting history on the Elephantine stele, or did he create a popular but fictitious Syrian as a scapegoat in his campaign for Egypt's throne?

We must also ask what happened to Queen Tausret at the end of her reign. She was possibly a woman in her thirties by this time. Did she die of natural causes unexpectedly, or did she lose her throne in a palace coup or on the battlefield? Was she—as seen by the anonymous artist in the Cairo Ostrakon (CG 25125) from this period (see fig. 2.6)—an Egyptian version of Jeanne d'Arc, trying to save her country from the invader? Alternatively, does this ostrakon represent that artist's view of Tausret combating Sethnakht himself? Or, does this ostrakon have nothing to do with the queen at all?

The woman in the ostrakon is dressed in the costume and headdress of an Egyptian queen, and she is shown firing arrows at what appears to be a pharaoh who is firing numerous arrows at her. Does this depict an actual situation, or is the message here as ambiguous as the Elephantine stele? These conjectures are interesting but, unfortunately, not one of them offers any evidence to support its case. Even as her origins remain hidden from us, so do the final chapters of Tausret's life.

Historical Epilogue

Sethnakht's own reign was not much longer than four years[87] and, at the end of it, his son Ramesses III usurped Tausret's tomb and buried his father there (see Figure 2.7, in insert, and Chapter 4). It was probably Ramesses who altered her cartouches and transformed her name and her figures into those of Sethnakht. The queen was deprived of her sarcophagus, and her mummy—if it still exists—has never been identified. Even as they tried to wipe out her presence in her own tomb, Sethnakht and his descendants must also have been responsible for the painting out of Tausret's reign, together with the reign of Amenmesse and, in some cases, that of Siptah.

To a great extent, the campaigns of Tausret's successors were effective: there were very few mementos of the queen left in the ancient records. Strangely, it was in Homer's reference as interpreted by the ninth-century Byzantine monk, George Syncellus, who lived in Constantinople, that one of the few references to Tausret was made after her life had ended—and even that note was inaccurate, her gender then being seen as male. Not until the nineteenth-, twentieth-, and twenty-first-century Egyptologists investigated her tomb, her temple, and her history could Tausret again take her rightful place as one of Egypt's pharaohs.

Tausret and Other Regnant Queens

There are a number of similarities between Tausret and the previous regnant queens, Sobekneferu and Hatshepsut: all of them had been royal wives before they became rulers. Sobekneferu and Hatshepsut used both female and male iconography and textual references to themselves, as Tausret did, and both Hatshepsut and Tausret made their first steps to power through the regency of a young male king who was not a child of their own. But, as well as these similarities, there are a number of differences between Tausret and the other female pharaohs. In contrast to Hatshepsut, Tausret became ruler only after the death of her protégé, and unlike Hatshepsut, she never shared a co-regency with the junior partner. Another deviation from Hatshepsut's protocol was that Tausret adopted a Strong Bull name—*Beloved of Maat*—which Hatshepsut never did. Each of these regnant queens had an individual pattern for her reign and this is how it should be, for each of them appears to have had an independent agenda.

3

Forgotten Treasures: Tausret as Seen in Her Monuments

CATHARINE H. ROEHRIG

Traditionally, the ancient Egyptians preferred to have a male ruler on the throne. The king was, after all, understood as the living Horus—and Horus was a male deity. The ideal king was understood to be a young man in the prime of life and, in general, the reigning king, no matter what his age or physical abilities, was portrayed in art as just that—a young man in the prime of life. Of course, from time to time, a child would succeed his father on the throne. From at least the middle of the 1st Dynasty in the Old Kingdom (c. 3000 BCE),[1] one of the contingency plans for this circumstance was to establish the king's mother (the *mwt nswt*) as regent for her son.[2] One suspects that this practice arose to avoid dynastic strife by ensuring a smooth transition when the young king came of age—a mother might be expected to give over power to her son whereas a male regent might not.[2] Whatever the reasoning, this practice continued through the Ptolemaic era, and it is possible to identify a number of queens who served in this capacity. Among them was Queen Ankhnesmeryre II, mother of Pepi II of the 6th Dynasty (c. 2246 BCE). Ankhnesmeryre is depicted in a charming statuette holding on her lap her young son, who is shown as a miniature king.[3] In Egyptian artistic convention, it is only in extraordinary circumstances that anyone but a deity is shown on a larger scale than the king. Thus, this small statue unequivocally portrays the power of this queen.

In the New Kingdom, there are two known cases in which the choice of a queen regent was modified. The first, in the 18th Dynasty, involves the accession of Thutmose III, whose mother was a secondary wife and not the principal wife (*ḥmt nswt wrt*) of his father, Thutmose II. The second, in the 19th Dynasty, involves the accession of Siptah, whose foreign-born mother appears to have been a king's wife, but again, not the principal wife. In these two cases, the mothers held no position of influence or authority when their sons took the throne, and neither acted officially on her son's behalf. Instead, the principal queen of the child's predecessor on the throne became regent for the young king. In the case of Thutmose III, this was his father's principal wife (and half-sister) Hatshepsut. In the case of Siptah, it was Tausret, the principal wife of Siptah's predecessor Seti II.

Although a queen might occasionally wield great influence during her son's or husband's reign, only a handful of women actually became rulers of Egypt in their own right. Probably the most famous of these female pharaohs is Cleopatra VII, the last of the Ptolemies. Her twenty-one-year reign ended in 30 BCE, when Egypt ceased to be an independent nation-state and became part of the Roman Empire. By far the most successful female ruler was Maatkare Hatshepsut of the 18th Dynasty who lived some 250 years before Tausret's time. Her twenty-one-year reign as senior co-ruler with her nephew, Thutmose III, ended in his apparently peaceful succession to sole rule in about 1458 BCE.

One difficulty in reconstructing the reigns of Egypt's female rulers is that their monuments were invariably attacked after their deaths and their names were generally omitted from later lists of kings. Although the historical record is not complete for either Hatshepsut or Cleopatra, their lengthy reigns have still provided modern historians with a large number of documents in the form of buildings, statuary, small objects, contemporary texts, and, in the case of Cleopatra, the writings of Classical historians. Unfortunately, for the women like Tausret who had briefer reigns, the contemporary historical record is much less complete and, thus, more open to speculative interpretation.

In the case of Tausret, we are fortunate to know her names and titles from various inscriptions (see Chapter 2), though most of these were altered, partially erased, or covered over in succeeding reigns. We are also fortunate to have a number of key monuments and artifacts that date to various significant periods of her public life. These material remains suggest that she played a prominent role in the royal court from early in the reign of her husband, Sety II.

Tausret as Queen: The First Building Phase of Her Tomb (KV 14)

The earliest datable monument dedicated to Tausret is her tomb, KV 14 in the royal cemetery we now call the Valley of the Kings (see Hartwig Altenmüller's discussion of the tomb in his chapter in this volume).[4] Although a number of 18th-Dynasty queens were provided with individual tombs in this cemetery,[5] Tausret was the only queen of the 19th Dynasty to be so honored. The tradition of her time, begun by the founder of the dynasty, Ramesses I, was to bury queens in a separate cemetery now known as the Valley of the Queens.

It should be noted that the tombs created for queens in both the 18th and 19th Dynasties had plans that were recognizably different from those of kings.[6]

Hartwig Altenmüller has shown that work on Tausret's tomb was initiated by Sety II[7] in the second year of his reign on the 8th day of the 1st month of *peret*.[8] The fact that her husband planned a burial for Tausret in what had become exclusively a king's cemetery suggests that very early on she played a more significant role in the court than that of most principal queens (*ḥmt nswt wrt* or "King's Great Wife").[9] In addition, the plan of Tausret's tomb has nothing in common with the known tombs of earlier 19th-Dynasty queens, to say nothing of their 18th-Dynasty predecessors.[10] Instead, the initial plan of Tausret's tomb is a small-scale version of the standard Ramesside king's tomb plan that was established by Merenptah.[11] Including the entrance, this plan has ten corridors and chambers along an absolutely straight axis that culminates in an eight-pillared burial chamber with a central section that has a depressed floor and a vaulted ceiling.[12]

One can only speculate as to why Tausret was accorded the great honor of having a tomb in the king's cemetery. This having been said, the suggestions made further on are based on the location of her tomb, its plan, and the fact that Tausret's husband, Sety II, was the son and heir of Merenptah. Despite Sety's apparently legitimate claim to the throne, the existence of Amenmesse, who claimed the titles of king before or even during Sety's reign (see Chapter 2), indicates that the dynastic succession was in question. This being the case, one wonders if Sety was honoring Tausret because of her own royal connections. Such connections, if they existed, are never explicitly stated. If Tausret were a daughter of Merenptah and a sister, or half-sister, of her husband, one would expect her to have the title "king's daughter" (*s3t nswt*) or "king's sister" (*snt nswt*), but neither title is found in any of her surviving inscriptions. Perhaps Tausret's connection was with Ramesses II, who had reigned for more than six decades before Merenptah, his thirteenth son, ascended the throne. If Tausret were the daughter of a crown prince who had been one of Merenptah's older brothers, or if she were a much younger daughter of Ramesses II himself, her own royal blood might have been seen as strengthening Sety's claim to the throne.

People generally assume that Tausret was the same age as or younger than her husband—but it is equally possible that she was some years older and had longer-standing connections with powerful officials in the court. If this were the case, she might have been a valuable advisor to the young king, who was probably younger than twenty when he came to the throne. The location of Tausret's tomb in the king's cemetery, and its plan—that of a king built on a slightly smaller scale—suggest that she may have played the role of a subordinate co-ruler with her husband—not simply the chief queen. Such a role could certainly have justified a small-scale "king's" tomb in the "king's" cemetery.

Even if Tausret were as much as ten or even fifteen years older than her husband, she would still have been of child-bearing age. Unfortunately, no male children of the couple, if they existed, were alive when Sety II died. Although the father of Sety's successor Siptah is still open to question, we know that Tausret was not his mother. However, probably because of her position as principal queen of Siptah's immediate predecessor, Tausret appears to have wielded significant power as the young king's regent.

Tausret as Regent: The Statue of Tausret Holding Siptah on Her Lap

Several monuments date to the time when Tausret was acting as regent and/ or counselor of the young king Siptah. Among the earliest is probably a statue now in the collection of the Staatliche Sammlung Ägyptische Kunst in Munich (GI. 122).[13] This work depicts the small figure of a king seated on the lap of an adult. The king wears a short kilt and sandals. His left arm rests on his left leg; his right arm is bent up across his chest. In his right hand he holds the crook and the flail which rest on his right shoulder. The king's head is missing so it is impossible to know what sort of crown he wore. He was certainly not wearing the *nemes*-headcloth, however, as there are no lappets visible on his shoulders. The king's feet rest on a tall stool projecting from the side of the statue. This foot rest is decorated on its sides with pairs of bound captives. On the front, above a device symbolizing the union of the two lands of Egypt are two columns of hieroglyphs. The right column begins with the title "Lord of the Two Lands" and the left with the epithet "Lord of Appearances," but the cartouches below have been erased. Although the most visible inscriptions on the statue have been destroyed, it is still possible to read a pair of small cartouches on the king's kilt. These identify him as Akhenre-Setepenre Merenptah-Siptah. As Siptah changed his name from Ramesses-Siptah to Merenptah-Siptah in the second year of his reign, the statue must date to Year 2 or later.

We know that the king represented in this statue is Siptah, but what of the adult? Unfortunately, this figure has been almost entirely chiseled away. Traces of the adult's legs survive at the front and on the left side of the statue, and it is possible to see that the individual wore sandals. There also appear to be traces of pleats near the back of the left ankle suggesting the standard long pleated garment worn by both men and women at this time. These details of dress identify the individual as human rather than divine.[14] The adult was seated on a low-backed throne with a cloth draped over the back. The sides of the throne are decorated with a device that signifies the union of Upper and Lower Egypt. This consists of papyrus and lotus plants tied around the hieroglyph *sm3*, which means "to unite." The same device is on the front of Siptah's foot rest mentioned earlier. This throne indicates that the adult was royal. Thus, although there is virtually nothing left of the adult figure, one can suggest with a fair amount of certainty that the royal adult holding Siptah on her lap was Tausret. This statue is a close parallel to the Old Kingdom statuette mentioned earlier that commemorates the role of Queen Ankhnesmeryre as regent for her son Pepi II, and a similar role for Tausret vis-à-vis Siptah is presumably commemorated here.[15]

Tausret as Regent: The Reliefs at the Temple of Amada

Another early piece of physical evidence from the time of Tausret's regency is from a small temple dedicated to Amun and Re-Horakhty at the site of Amada, in Nubia.[16] The temple had originally been built and decorated by Thutmose III and his immediate successors in the 18th Dynasty, but its decoration was damaged during the reign of Akhenaten when the name of Amun was erased. In the 19th Dynasty, Sety I, Ramesses II, and Merenptah made some restorations and added their own texts.

More work was conducted on the temple in the reign of Siptah, and this was commemorated by reliefs and texts that form the lowest register of the jambs on either side of the door leading into the temple. On the right jamb is the standing figure of Tausret, facing left, holding two sistra in front of her. She is dressed in sandals and the long, full garments of the time, and she wears the vulture headdress and modius of a queen. She faces a column of text that identifies her as the "God's Wife of Amun, the King's Great Wife, Lady of the Two Lands, Tausret-beloved-of-Mut, justified." The corner of the jamb is damaged so the beginning of this inscription with the name of the god Amun is missing, but the rest of the inscription and the figure of the queen are intact.

On the left jamb is the kneeling figure of a man with both arms raised in a worshipful pose. He is dressed in a long robe and sandals. Above his head is a line of hieroglyphs that identifies him as the sole friend and chancellor, Bay, who faces two columns of text written above the device symbolizing the union of the two lands. The first column names the "Lord of the Two Lands, Akhenre-Setepenre" and the second reads "Lord of Appearances, Merenptah-Siptah." As with the inscription naming Tausret, the one naming Bay is intact except at the beginning where the stone jamb itself is weathered.

It is interesting that Tausret and Bay are pictured, but not the king himself. This implies that it is these two who are in charge, suggesting that the king is still too young to rule in his own right. Thus, these reliefs appear to date to an early stage of Tausret's regency, but after Year 2 when the king changed his name from Ramesses-Siptah to Merenptah-Siptah. The vignettes and texts were carved on blank areas of the jambs below the 18th-Dynasty reliefs. The differences between these two vignettes are significant. They could have been symmetrical, one standing figure on each side of the door, but they are not.

Although the kneeling figure of Bay is about the same scale as the standing figure of Tausret, the area taken up by his figure and the accompanying text is smaller. Tausret is shown standing as she goes into the presence of the god, whereas Bay is shown kneeling in front of the cartouches of the king. This is a fitting artistic representation of their difference in status: the royal queen, who is also "God's Wife of Amun," versus the official who serves the king.

Tausret as Regent: The Second Building Phase of KV 14

Although Tausret's tomb was initiated in the reign of her husband, Sety II, none of the decoration appears to date to his reign. This may seem odd, but one must remember that, during the eight to nine years between the death of Merenptah (c. 1203 BCE) and the accession of Siptah (c. 1194 BCE), three tombs were being worked on in the Valley of the Kings, and Tausret's tomb was probably not the priority.

Decoration of the tomb began during the reign of Siptah and the first interior corridor was executed in fine sunk relief and painted. On either side of this corridor Tausret is most often shown alone, offering to various gods, but the central scene on the south wall depicts Siptah offering alone. The king is represented as a physically fit adult man in the prime of life as would be expected, whatever his age at the time, and despite his physical deformity (see Chapter 2). The most interesting decoration in this corridor is the central scene on the north wall that depicts Siptah with Tausret following behind and both offering to the god Geb (Figure 4.4.). This juxtaposition of a male and female royal figure is significant as it occurs in no other royal tomb in the Valley during this or any other dynasty. As a general rule, queens do not appear in their husband's tombs,[17] nor do kings appear in the tombs of their queens.[18] Later in the 19th Dynasty, in the tombs of princes, the king is often the dominant figure preceding his son into the presence of various gods, introducing the prince or interceding on his behalf. In these scenes, the prince is playing a subordinate and passive role.[19]

The offering scene on the north wall of KV 14 is similar to scenes that sometimes appear on temple walls where the king and queen, or two co-rulers in the case of Hatshepsut and Thutmose III in the Chapel Rouge, are shown together offering to gods. Although Tausret is depicted in the secondary position when she appears with Siptah in this scene in her tomb, she is being treated as a participating rather than a passive member of the scene. This iconography, unique in a funerary context, could well be intended to represent the reality of Siptah as the reigning king and Tausret as his regent and advisor. Interestingly, in this scene, Tausret is depicted with a short hairstyle, but a thick side-lock hangs over her shoulder and down her back. This hairstyle could be interpreted as an indication of her own royal descent.[20]

Sometime, probably near the end of Siptah's life, Tausret appears to have planned an addition to her tomb (see Chapter 4). This took the form of a second, standard-size burial chamber that would have been just beyond the first (Chamber J in Figure 4.1).[21] Only the beginnings of this room (K1a, K1b) had been excavated when Siptah died near the end of his sixth year

Tombs in the Valley of the Kings from Tausret's Time

KV 15   The tomb of Sety II, if completed, would have been as large as that of his father Merenptah (KV 8). However, when Sety died, excavation of the tomb had proceeded only to a point just beyond the first pillared hall (usually designated F). The tomb is decorated throughout, though only the figures and text at the front of the tomb were executed in relief. The bulk of the decoration was simply painted on the tomb walls.

KV 10   The tomb of Amenmesse may have gone through some redesign in the late 20th Dynasty, but it was certainly completed through the pillared hall (F) during Amenmesse's reign. The second and third corridors are shorter than normal, but otherwise the rooms were excavated at the standard scale for a king's tomb. Only the entrance and first corridor appear to have decoration dating to Amenmesse's reign.

KV 14   The original plan of Tausret's tomb would have been about two-thirds the size of a standard king's tomb. The later additions of corridors and a second, standard-size burial chamber made the final tomb roughly the same length as other kings' tombs of the period.

KV 47   The plan of Siptah's tomb was based on the standard king's tomb established by Merenptah. The entrance and the following corridors were cut into good quality limestone and the first section of the tomb is beautifully decorated with a combination of painting and painted relief. Unfortunately, the second half of the tomb was carved into poor quality stone, and during the excavation of the burial chamber, KV 47 ran into an 18th-Dynasty tomb. As a result, the tomb plan was revised. The original burial chamber was redesigned as a corridor and a new burial chamber, with a slightly modified plan, was excavated beyond.

KV 13   Another pseudo-royal tomb was also being excavated during Tausret's time as regent. This was the tomb of the chancellor Bay, whose power seems to have been greatest early in the reign of Siptah. This tomb is similar in scale to the original tomb of Tausret and probably was intended to have had a similar plan, though it was not completed.

(see Chapter 4). It is likely that this burial chamber was not completed for two reasons: the work had run into a large fault line that caused a crack in the ceiling, and the death of Siptah and installation of Tausret as sole ruler allowed for (or perhaps demanded) a grander expansion of the tomb

Tausret as Ruler: The Headless Statue from Medinet Nasr

The only surviving image that we know was created specifically to portray Tausret as ruler of Egypt is a statue that was discovered at Medinet Nasr, on the outskirts of Cairo (Figures 2.3 and 3.1). In 1971, this area, approximately six kilometers (3.72 miles) southeast of the city center, was being developed as a new residential district and ground was being broken for a park when a bulldozer uncovered some pharaonic artifacts. The most significant object was a headless statue of a seated woman identified by the inscriptions as Tausret. A description of the statue accompanied by photographs and transcriptions of the texts was published by Egyptian Egyptologist Hassan S.K. Bakry.[22]

The statue is approximately life size[23] and depicts Tausret seated on a block throne with a back pillar. On her head, she must have worn a *nemes*-headcloth, the lappets of which are visible on her shoulders, and around her neck is a broad collar. She also wears sandals on her feet and a long pleated garment that leaves only her ankles, left hand, and right forearm uncovered. The cloth reveals the contours of her torso, clearly indicating her feminine breasts, and her navel is visible above the belt around her hips. From the sides, her calves are clearly visible through the pleats, but heavy folds of cloth at the front of the skirt form a triangular panel that hides her knees and lower legs when the statue is seen head on (Figure 3.1).

In sculpture of the 19th Dynasty, the garments worn by men and women are quite similar. However, there are several easily discernible differences that clearly identify the garments depicted on this statue as those of a man. A woman's pleated dress of this period would normally fall to her heels, covering her ankles, and there would be no panel of fabric at the front of the skirt. Instead, the pleated cloth would reveal the outline of her legs both at the sides and in the front.

The fact that Tausret wears masculine attire should not be taken as an indication that she is pretending to be a man—after all, her breasts are clearly indicated beneath the garment's folds as they would be if she were wearing feminine attire. Rather, she is wearing the costume appropriate for the accoutrements of a king. Suspended from her belt is an apron that hangs down over her knees. The apron's hem is decorated with six *uraeus*-cobras, each with a sun disk on its head. This apron would drape far more gracefully (and comfortably) over the thick front folds of a man's skirt than over the sheerer, more clinging skirt of a woman.

FIGURE 3.1 Front view of the Statue of Tausret from Medinet Nasr. Drawing by Scott Murphy after pl. II in Hassan S. K. Bakry, "The Discovery of a Statue of Queen Twosre (1202–1194? BCE) at Madinet Nasr, Cairo."

The inscriptions on the statue, which are all intact, give Tausret's titulary as ruler of Egypt (for this titulary, see the Inset Box in Chapter 2). For most kings, this consisted of five names: the Horus name, which usually began *Strong-bull*; the Nebty name (literally "He/She of the Two Ladies" meaning the goddesses of Upper and Lower Egypt); the Golden Horus name; the throne name (or prenomen, taken at the king's accession); and the personal name (or nomen—the name that was given at birth). The last two names are the ones that are most commonly used and each appears within a cartouche.

On the Medinet Nasr statue, only four names are recorded for Tausret. In fact, none of her surviving monuments records her golden Horus name, though this may simply be an accident of preservation. However, if she had a golden Horus name, it does seem odd that it is not recorded on this statue with the other four, three of which are repeated several times and accompanied by various epithets as seen below. In the following translations, epithets and titles are written in standard text, Tausret's official names are in italics, and missing text is written between brackets.[24]

On the back pillar Tausret is identified as

[Living? Horus] *Strong-bull-beloved-of-Maat*, King of Upper and Lower Egypt who is installed by Re, Lord of the Two Lands *Daughter-of-Re-beloved-of-Amun* (more often written in its ancient Egyptian form Sitre-Meryamun), Son of Re, Lord of Appearances like Atum *Daughter-of-Re-beloved-of-Amun*, beloved of Hathor-lady-of-the-red-mountain

Around the left side of the base Tausret is identified as

Living Horus *Strong-bull-beloved-of-Maat*, Two Ladies *Who-sets-Egypt-in-order-and-subdues-foreign-lands*, King of Upper and Lower Egypt, *Daughter-of-Re-beloved-of-Amun*, Son of Re *Tausret-chosen-of-Mut* (more often written Tausret-Setepenmut), beloved of Hathor-lady-of-the-red-mountain

Around the right side of the base she is described as

Living Horus *Strong-bull-beloved-of-Maat*, Beautiful lord as king like Atum, King of Upper and Lower Egypt, *Daughter-of-Re-beloved-of-Amun*, Son of Re *Tausret-chosen-of-Mut*, beloved of Hathor-lady-of-the-red-mountain

Most of the titles and epithets in these inscriptions are in the masculine form—for example, "Son of Re," but this should not be taken as an attempt on Tausret's part to be understood as a man. Her two cartouche names, those most commonly written on monuments, clearly state her feminine gender. Her throne name, Sitre-Meryamun, begins with the feminine "Daughter of Re" (Sitre). Her personal name, Tausret-Setepenmut, includes the feminine name she was given at birth, Tausret, and the phrase "chosen of Mut" (Setepenmut), which associates her with a powerful goddess who is often included in the names of queens.[25] Most of her male predecessors, beginning with Ramesses II, used the phrase "chosen of Re" (Setepenre), thus associating themselves with a god.

In the inscriptions on the Medinet Nasr statue, Tausret is described several times as "beloved of Hathor, Lady of the Red Mountain." The red mountain in question is near the site where the statue was found and has a similar name today, *el-Gebel el-Ahmar* ("the red mountain" in Arabic)—a place that is noted for its quarries. Quartzite from this area had been employed by generations of Egyptian pharaohs, including Ramesses II who commemorated his use of the

The Seated Statue of Ramesses II in Turin

Another parallel to Tausret's Medinet Nasr statue is a seated statue
of Ramesses II in the Egyptian Museum in Turin. Although similar in
type, this greater than life-size statue differs in several respects. The
Turin statue, which still has its head, depicts Ramesses wearing the blue
crown (*kheperesh*) instead of the *nemes*-headcloth. Ramesses is dressed
in the typical long, pleated garments of a king, but he wears no apron
decorated with *uraeus*-cobras. Like Tausret, Ramesses holds his right
arm bent up across his chest, but, as on his Cairo statue, he holds only
the crook in his right hand—not the crook and flail as does Tausret.
Ramesses rests his left arm on his left leg and he holds a cloth in his left
fist, whereas Tausret's left hand lies open with the palm down.

quarries in a stela now in Cairo (CG 34504).[26] It is certainly not surprising that
Tausret's statue was also made of quartzite from these quarries.[27]

The pose and iconography of Tausret's headless statue was undoubtedly
influenced by those of earlier kings, in particular, two that depict Ramesses II:
one in the Museo Egizio in Turin, Italy,[28] and the other in the Egyptian Museum,
Cairo (CG 42140).[29] Tausret's statue bears a closer resemblance to the Cairo
statue of Ramesses II which, as it happens, is also missing the head. At a preserved height of only 67 cm (26.4 inches), this statue is smaller than life size.
It represents Ramesses dressed in the same pleated garments and sandals as
Tausret. He also wears the *nemes*-headcloth, and an apron decorated with cobras
falls over his knees. Like Tausret, Ramesses has his right arm bent across his
chest; however, whereas Tausret holds both the crook and flail across her right
shoulder, Ramesses holds only the crook.[30] It is perhaps unwise to read too
much into this difference as there are examples of other kings holding both the
crook and flail or just the crook.[31] However, it is interesting to note that the flail,
albeit a somewhat different form of flail, is an accoutrement of the principal
queen, and perhaps Tausret is combining the symbols of both king and queen
in this instance (see the discussion of the final phase of KV 14 later in the chapter). Unfortunately, the right shoulder of the Medinet Nasr statue is broken and
it is impossible to tell from the published photographs whether the type of flail
can be determined, although it appears to be the stiff-handled flail of a king.

Another interesting difference between the Medinet Nasr and Cairo statues
is that Ramesses holds an *ankh* in his left hand. This hieroglyph, symbolizing
life, is an attribute usually reserved for the gods, and its presence suggests that
we see here the deified king. The statue of Ramesses was found in the famous
cachette of statues in the temple of Amun at Karnak, and the inscription indicates that it was set up in some part of this temple. Based on its inscriptions,
the statue of Tausret was also intended for a temple—this one dedicated to
Hathor-lady-of-the-red-mountain near Heliopolis.

The Medinet Nasr statue is significant not only because it unequivocally depicts Tausret as a female pharaoh but also because it records her Nebty name "the one who sets Egypt in order and subdues foreign lands." This is similar to the Nebty name of Ramesses II, which was also adopted by her husband Sety II (see the Inset Box in chapter 2 on Tausret's titulary). Thus, it is possible that Tausret was associating herself with her most powerful predecessor (who may also have been her father or grandfather), and/or with her husband, who becomes a significant presence in her tomb. However, the name may have been chosen because it reflected the troubled times in which Tausret ruled. Considering the dynastic problems encountered by her husband Sety II vis-à-vis Amenmesse, followed by Siptah's possibly ambiguous claim to the throne, Tausret may quite literally have had to "set Egypt in order" and "subdue foreign lands."

Tausret as Ruler: Inscribed Material from Western Asia

In October 1961, H. J. Franken of Leiden University published an article on the second season of work at Deir 'Alla, a site in Jordan roughly midway between the Dead Sea and the Sea of Galilee. During this season, he and his team had discovered a fragmentary faience vase inscribed with a royal name he read as Usermaatre-Setepenre, the throne name of Ramesses II.[32] The next year, French Egyptologist Jean Yoyotte wrote an article in which he corrected the reading of this name to Tausret-Setepenmut, the extended personal name of Tausret.[33] This jar fragment is not the only evidence of Tausret as pharaoh in the Near East. In 2005, an excavation at Sidon on the coast of Lebanon, sponsored by the British Museum, turned up three fragments of a faience jar with a more complete set of Tausret's cartouche names and a string of epithets such as "Lady of Strength" (or might, or power- *nbt ḥpš*), "Lady of Action" (*nbt irt* [*ḥt*]), and "Who Subdues Foreign Lands" (*w'f ḥ3swt*)—part of her Two Ladies name, which appears to be used here simply as another epithet that emphasizes her strength.[34]

In his article about the Sidon find, Marcel Marée suggests that these two vases and another from a temple of Hathor at Timna were all diplomatic gifts to local temples that served to promote goodwill and solidify alliances in difficult times. Such gifts, with Tausret's names as pharaoh, indicate that she moved quickly on this diplomatic front after taking on the responsibilities of sole ruler.

Tausret as Ruler: The Naophorous Statue of the High Priest of Ptah Iyri in Paris

In his article on the fragmentary vase from Deir 'Alla, Yoyotte mentions a limestone naophorous statue in the Musée du Louvre in Paris (A 71) depicting a

High Priest of Ptah at Memphis named Iyri.[35] This statue is of interest because of the cartouches on the man's shoulders. On his left shoulder is the personal name of Sety II, *Sety-Merenptah*. On the right shoulder is the extended personal name of Tausret, *Tausret-Setepenmut*—a name she does not seem to use in any other context while she is queen. Yoyotte puts forward two possibilities. The first is that Tausret took the epithet "chosen of Mut" even before Sety's death, a possibility that he discards as there is no other evidence for her having done so. The second possibility he puts forward is that the inscriptions on Iyri's statue commemorate the association Tausret makes between herself and Sety after she becomes sole ruler, as shown in the altered decoration of her tomb. This latter seems the more likely explanation. A number of New Kingdom statues in the Egyptian Museum in Cairo have a king's cartouche inscribed on only one shoulder—and this is always the right shoulder.[36] Tausret's cartouche is on Iyri's right shoulder, which suggests to me that she, not Sety II, is regarded as the dominant royal figure here. It seems unlikely that the name of Sety II would have been inscribed on Iyri's left shoulder during Sety's reign and that of Tausret added later.

An inscription with an offering text for the royal *ka* of Tausret was discovered at Memphis,[37] the center of the worship of Ptah, so it is not surprising that a high priest of this god would have been represented in a statue with Tausret's cartouche on his shoulder.

Tausret as Ruler: Her Temple of Millions of Years

Once she became ruler of Egypt in her own right, Tausret built a temple (a monument for the afterlife which nevertheless began to function during the monarch's reign) for herself at the edge of the cultivation in western Thebes. This strip of desert had been used for royal temples by generations of New Kingdom pharaohs since the early 18th Dynasty. Tausret chose an empty site midway between the temples of Merenptah to the south and Thutmose IV (an 18th-Dynasty king) to the north. It is unfortunate that virtually no decoration remains from this temple, but renewed excavations at the site have revealed important information that is discussed by Richard Wilkinson in his chapter in this volume.

Tausret as Ruler: The Final Phase of KV 14 as Tausret's Tomb

After the death of Siptah, Tausret once again adapted her tomb in the Valley of the Kings to her new circumstances. What had been the beginnings of a new, larger burial chamber was adapted into a corridor (K1 on Figure 4.1) with two unfinished side chambers (K1a, b). This and a second corridor (K2)[38] led to a

FIGURE 1.1 The 4th-Dynasty queen Hetepheres II, consort of Snefru: the earliest known representation of a queen taking the form of a protective sphinx. Photograph by John Bodsworth.

FIGURE 1.2 Hatshepsut presents herself as a stereotypical pharaoh with an idealized man's body and wearing masculine clothes. From the wall of the Red Chapel, Karnak Temple of Amun. Photograph by Steven Snape.

FIGURE 1.3 Ramesses III and an unnamed queen, on the wall of the Temple of Medinet Habu. Photograph by Steven Snape.

FIGURE 1.4 The goddess Isis: the ultimate protective queen, wife, and mother. The "throne" sign that represents both her name and her headdress emphasizes the link between this goddess and the pharaoh. From Theodore Davis, *The Tomb of Siptah*, London, 1908.

FIGURE 1.5 Tetradrachem of Cleopatra VII. The Classical authors tell us that Cleopatra's charm lay in her voice and her intelligence; modern artists have assumed that she must also have been beautiful. From the Collection of the Garstang Museum, University of Liverpool. Photograph by Steven Snape.

FIGURE 2.7 A double scene originally showing Tausret led before Osiris by Horus and Anubis in the first hall of the queen's tomb. The queen's images have been deleted (at far left and far right) and the cartouches of her successor, Sethnakht, inscribed in their place. Photograph by Richard H. Wilkinson.

FIGURE 3.3 One of a pair of gold earrings from KV 56 with the Cartouche of Sety II. Painting by Harold Jones. From plate 7 in Theodore M. Davis et al., *The Tomb of Siphtah*. London, 1908.

FIGURE 3.4 Necklace from KV 56 in the Valley of the Kings. Theodore M. Davis Collection, Bequest of Theodore M. Davis, MMA30.8.66. Photograph by Gustavo Camps, courtesy of the Metropolitan Museum of Art.

FIGURE 4.5 Gods of the Judgment Hall of Osiris in Chamber I of Tausret's tomb. The vertical bands with the cartouches of Sethnakht between the deities overlie figures of Tausret originally painted in these locations. Photograph courtesy of the Tausret Project, University of Hamburg.

FIGURE 4.6 North wall of Burial Chamber J in the tomb of Tausret with a monumental depiction of the final scene of the "Book of Caverns." Photograph courtesy of the Tausret Project, University of Hamburg.

FIGURE 5.2 W. M. Flinders Petrie excavating a short distance from the Tausret temple site in 1896. A watercolor by Henry Wallis (EDC2674). Photograph courtesy of UCL Art Collections, University College London.

FIGURE A.1 An *Iunmutef* priest performs part of the "Opening of the Mouth" ritual of symbolic afterlife revivification before the figure of Tausret which has been erased by her successors in the queen's tomb. Photograph by Richard H. Wilkinson.

new burial chamber (L).[39] These three elements were excavated on the same scale as a standard king's tomb of the period, not the smaller scale of her original tomb. Another corridor (L2)[40] was started beyond the second burial chamber, but this was never completed. With all these new additions, the length of Tausret's tomb (KV 14, 158.41 meters) is nearly the same as the tomb of Merenptah (KV 8, 164.86 meters) and longer than the tomb of Siptah (KV 47, 124.93 meters).[41]

The decoration in the front half of the original KV 14 (A-J) was also adapted to Tausret's changed circumstances. The names in the texts accompanying the figures of Siptah were changed to Sety II, and most of the figures of Tausret herself were adapted to reflect her new powers (see Chapter 4). It is interesting that Tausret did not erase the figures of the male king in this part of her tomb and replace them with her own image or that of a god. She was, after all, the sole ruler of Egypt, not regent for or co-ruler with another king. In a more public place perhaps she might have needed the reference to her predecessors in order to promote her legitimacy—but why would this be necessary in her tomb?

As suggested elsewhere in this volume (see Chapter 2), it is possible that Tausret intended to rebury her husband, Sety II, in her tomb, and therefore, his image needed to be present. However, the male king, whether identified as Siptah or Sety II, was never depicted or named in the lower reaches of the tomb where the standard underworld texts typical of a king's tomb appear.[42] Aside from this, Sety II had his own tomb in the Valley of the Kings (KV 15), albeit a rather truncated one, and the funerary decoration therein was adapted to his use. His tomb was in the same vicinity as Tausret's tomb, so there seems to be no reason for her to have moved his body into KV 14, especially as she did not adapt any of the texts for his use.[43]

Another possible reason for the presence of the male king in Tausret's tomb is that she appears never to have entirely given up her role as queen. Although many of her images are adapted and her titles and names are altered, there are places in the tomb where she still appears as the *ḥmt nswt wrt* or "King's Great Wife" Tausret. Even in her altered images where she is identified by her king's names and titles, she holds a flail. This instrument can be the symbol of a queen as well as that of a king, although the two flails are different—and in at least one image in the first corridor of her tomb, the flail Tausret holds is the queen's flail, sometimes called a lily scepter or a fly-whisk scepter. In this version of the scene, she also wears the blue crown of a king, thus combining accoutrements of both royal offices (Figure 4.2, center).

For the ancient Egyptians, the concept of divine kingship was paralleled by a concept of divine queenship.[44] Although the king had by far the dominant role, in order to perform all of his ritual functions he required a queen. When the ruler was a female, someone still needed to perform the ritual role of queen. In the case of Hatshepsut, her daughter Neferure took on some of the titles of a queen, such as God's Wife, and presumably performed the ritual function of the queen vis-à-vis her mother. In the case of Tausret, there appears to have been no daughter and, perhaps, Tausret filled the double role of king and queen, at least for ritual purposes.

Tausret as Regent/Ruler: The Sarcophagus of Tausret Found in KV 13

While working in the tomb of Chancellor Bay, Hartwig Altenmüller discovered a granite sarcophagus with altered inscriptions that named prince Amenherkhepeshef, a son of Ramesses III of the early 20th Dynasty (Figure 4.7A and 4.7B).[45] It was Ramesses III who altered Tausret's tomb for his father Sethnakht, the king who was Tausret's successor on the throne. More than the inscriptions on the sarcophagus had required alteration for Amenherkhepeshef. The original owner had worn a lapped wig and the vulture crown of a queen. To adapt this for a prince, the left lappet was carved away, the right lappet was fashioned into the curled side-lock appropriate to a prince, the wings and tail of the vulture crown were largely polished away, and the vulture's head was removed.

Fortunately, the name of the owner, Tausret, is preserved on the foot of the lid. This sarcophagus appears to have been created for Tausret while she was queen or regent, and it has been suggested that she would have made a more kingly sarcophagus when she became pharaoh. While this is certainly possible, I would suggest that this sarcophagus may well have been the only sarcophagus made by Tausret. Although she did add a standard-size burial chamber to her tomb and adapted a number of the images in the first half of her original tomb to reflect her status as ruler, some of her images as queen were never altered. In her tomb, and even in the Medinet Nasr statue mentioned above, she always portrays herself as a female pharaoh. Thus, it seems unlikely to me that she would have created for herself a king's sarcophagus similar to those of Merenptah (in KV 8), Sety II (in KV 15), Siptah (in KV 47), or the one usurped for Sethnakht (in the second burial chamber of KV 14).[46] Tausret appears to have had some ambivalence when it came to changing her identity from "queen" to "king," or perhaps she saw no need to make a complete change. Whatever the case, she may have been quite happy to keep the original sarcophagus, queen's titles and all.[47]

Tausret as Queen, Regent, Ruler: The Cache of Jewelry in KV 56

On January 5, 1908, British excavator Edward R. Ayrton, working for American financier Theodore M. Davis, discovered a pit tomb (KV 56) near the central

Valley of the Kings.[48] During clearance of the tomb chamber, Ayrton uncovered a number of intact stone and pottery vessels. One vase of Egyptian alabaster was inscribed with the throne name of Ramesses II inlaid in blue paste. Another alabaster vase was inscribed with both cartouches of Tausret's husband, Sety II, also inlaid with blue paste. Against one wall was a pottery vessel that contained fragments of faience vases inscribed with the names of Sety II. There were also fragments of alabaster vessels, one with the names of Ramesses II and another with the names of Sety II. More interesting, however, was an astonishing trove of jewelry that included a number of pieces inscribed with the names of Sety II and Tausret as queen.

The objects from the jewelry cache that are of most interest to us are those inscribed with the names of Tausret and her husband. These include a wide finger ring, made of gold and glass or stone inlay (Cairo, CG 52261). This is decorated with a falcon, its wings outspread, the tips touching a vertical cartouche enclosing the throne name of Sety II. There were also thirteen rectangular plaques of gold foil embossed with double cartouches surmounted with plumes and enclosing the names of Sety II (Cairo, CG 52684). George Daressy, who wrote the catalogue of the finds, suggested that these plaques might have been part of a girdle.[49]

Two cuff-bracelets mentioned in Chapter 2 of Daressy's catalogue (Cairo, CG 52577-8; Figure 3.2) are both decorated with the same scene that depicts Sety II at the right, seated on a high-backed wooden chair, holding a cup in his left hand and a scepter in his right that is made of a *djed*-pillar, meaning "stability," and a device that means "millions of years." At the left stands Tausret holding a lotus in her right hand and a vase in her left hand from which she is about to pour liquid into the king's cup. On these two bracelets, Tausret is clearly identified as the King's Great Wife Tausret. The head coverings of the king and queen are quite similar, with both wearing a uraeus on the brow. Their hair or headcloths are a bit difficult to interpret, but the queen seems to wear something akin to a *nemes*-headcloth, except that the striations on the lappets are vertical rather than horizontal, suggesting hair.

There also appears to be a set of jewelry consisting of a diadem of rosettes (Cairo, CG 52644), a large pair of earrings decorated with similar rosettes and pendant cornflower blossoms (Cairo, CG 52397; Figure 3.3, see insert), and a necklace that was made up of filigree cornflower blossoms and ball beads (Cairo, CG 52679, MMA 30.8.66; Figure 3.4, see insert).[50] The rosettes on the earrings are inscribed with the cartouches of Sety II. The rosettes of the diadem are inscribed with Sety's cartouches and also with the simple queen's cartouche of Tausret. This is significant because most of the inscribed jewelry of a royal woman, whether princess or queen, records the name of the king who gave it, not the woman who wore it.[51]

Other jewelry in the cache also records Tausret's name. A penannular earring of gold and glass or stone inlay is inscribed with her name in a cartouche

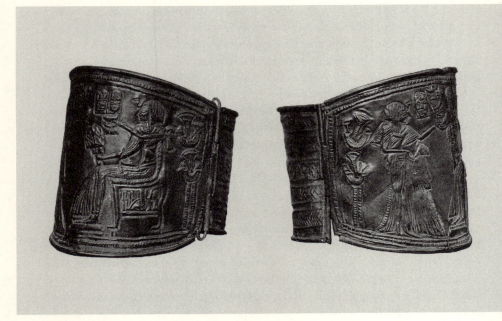

FIGURE 3.2 Two views of a cuff bracelet from KV 56 (now in Cairo). Adapted from a photograph on plate 10 in Theodore M. Davis et al., *The Tomb of Siphtah*. London, 1908.

surmounted with two falcon feathers (Cairo, CG 52331), and a double finger ring of gold is composed of two cartouches enclosing the name Tausret and surmounted by two ostrich plumes (Cairo, CG 52246). It is interesting that Tausret's personal name is associated both with the two falcon feathers, which decorate the *šwty*-crown worn by queens, and with the two ostrich plumes that decorate the *atef*-crown worn by gods, the king, and also the God's Wife of Amun.

The other jewelry in the cache may well have belonged to Tausret, but, with the exception of a ring recording the name of Ramesses II, it is uninscribed and could have come from another burial, so it will not be discussed here. The tomb in which the jewelry was discovered, KV 56, is a type that can be dated to the 18th Dynasty, but the chamber is oddly shaped, suggesting that the tomb was unfinished, and there is no evidence that it was ever used during this period. There are two theories as to why a group of objects from the 19th Dynasty were found in this 18th-Dynasty tomb. The first, suggested in the publication of the tomb, is that these objects were stashed, at the time when Tausret's tomb was usurped for the burial of Sethnakht, either for safekeeping, or as part of a robber's haul.[52]

A second interpretation was put forward by Cyril Aldred, who suggested that the objects were the remains of the intact burial of a child—probably a daughter of Tausret and Sety II.[53] The basis for this was an area near the jewelry that was scattered with the remains of gilded stucco interspersed with inlays and faience hair curls that are typical of coffin decoration. Also important for Aldred's argument was the presence of a small silver sandal and a pair of silver "gloves," both suggestive of funerary trappings. In addition, the silver "gloves" contained eight of the gold rings, including those inscribed with the names of Sety II, Tausret, and Ramesses II.[54]

Although Aldred's suggestion is intriguing, Ayrton's description of the tomb argues against this being an intact burial.[55] Ayrton states that the shaft was filled with washed-in debris and the chamber was encumbered with more or less the same material to a depth of up to forty-one inches. He cleared this debris in level sections and found the stone and pottery objects lying on a layer of what he thought was an accumulation of dust some six to twelve inches thick that had been solidified by water coming into the tomb. He thought this bottom layer had accumulated while the tomb had lain open before the 19th-Dynasty objects were introduced.

No evidence of mud sealing around the chamber door was noted either by the Davis team or by members of the Amarna Royal Tombs Project when the tomb was re-cleared.[56] An official burial or a later reburial would surely have been sealed, protecting it from water-borne debris, if not from dampness. But the gold jewelry appears to have been embedded in compacted mud, and the same mud filled the silver "gloves." Also, not a single scrap of bone was ever found in the tomb. Even if the burial had been that of a child, one would expect to have found teeth or part of the skull, or an end of one of the long bones of the arms or legs. No such evidence of burial was ever discovered. If it were a burial that had been entered in ancient times, it is inconceivable that a trove of gold jewelry would have been left in place.

So, what is the source of the gold jewelry in the tomb? It is quite possible that Tausret would have made use of her queen's jewelry throughout her career: first as principal queen; then as regent for Siptah; and finally as ruler. After all, her position as queen and regent derived from her being (or having been) the *hmt nswt wrt* of Sety II, and it is clear from the final decoration phase of her tomb that even as ruler she continued to derive strength from her association with her husband. The pieces of inscribed jewelry may have been prized possessions that she wore on ceremonial occasions.[57] They are certainly the kinds of items that she would have included in her tomb.

It is possible, as Daressy suggested, that the jewelry and other material in KV 56 was removed from KV 14 when Ramesses III usurped it for his father. But, the objects in the KV 56—gold jewelry, which may or may not all have come from the same tomb; a tiny silver sandal, too small for anyone but a young child; two small silver "gloves" that would have fit over the hands of a child or a small woman; gilded stucco, faience curls, and other inlays that suggest a decorated coffin lid—appear to come from more than one burial. The cuff bracelets have been badly crushed, suggesting very rough treatment, and the rings could have been placed in the gloves for easier carrying. This suggests to me a robber's cache rather than a careful reburial of goods. On the other hand, the pottery jar containing broken faience and alabaster vessels inscribed with the names of kings look more like a cleanup effort than a robbery. So, the question of how objects inscribed with the names of Sety II and Tausret came to be in an 18th-Dynasty pit tomb remains unanswered.

Conclusion

From the excavation of the monuments discussed here, we have only limited evidence on which to reconstruct the life of Tausret as queen, regent, and ruler. What impresses me most is that Tausret appears to pointedly retain her feminine identity even when she becomes pharaoh. Her statue from Medinet Nasr and the images in her tomb clearly represent a woman wielding the power of a king. Perhaps this is because she had such a short sole reign. Had she ruled as long as Hatshepsut, perhaps her images would have taken on the aspect of the ideal Egyptian king—a young man in the prime of life. Perhaps not. After all, she was not living in the same world as Hatshepsut, and circumstances may have required something different from a female ruler.

As had happened to Hatshepsut some two centuries earlier, most of Tausret's monuments were destroyed or altered by her successors, and she was omitted from later king lists. However, again as with Hatshepsut, at least the cultural memory of Tausret's reign was preserved. To the ancient Egyptians, a female ruler, however long or short her reign, would have been extraordinary— someone worthy of stories to be passed on by word of mouth, from generation to generation. Perhaps this is why both rulers have a place in the history of Egypt written by Manetho in the time of the first Ptolemies, some eight hundred years after Tausret's death. In the case of Hatshepsut, Manetho records the twenty-year reign of a female ruler in the middle of the 18th Dynasty. In the case of Tausret, he records the seven-year reign of a king Thouris at the end of the 19th Dynasty. Unlike Hatshepsut, Tausret may also figure in the tales of Homer, as noted by Gae Callender at the beginning of Chapter 2 in this volume.

4

A Queen in a Valley of Kings: The Tomb of Tausret

HARTWIG ALTENMÜLLER

Exploration of the Tomb

The tomb of Queen Tausret (KV 14) is one of the largest decorated tombs in the Valley of the Kings in Thebes—a fact that is all the more impressive considering that Tausret was one of only very few women, and of only two ruling queens, to be buried in the royal valley. The tomb was cut 112 meters (367.45 feet) deep into the cliffs of a small western branch of the valley and belongs to a cluster of four monuments from the late 19th Dynasty: the tombs of Tausret (KV 14), Sety II (KV 15), Chancellor Bay (KV 13), and Siptah (KV 47).

Tausret's tomb has lain open since classical antiquity, as is attested by a two-lined Greek graffito recently discovered in one of the corridors. However, the first detailed reports about the tomb are from the late eighteenth century. Richard Pococke produced the first plan of the tomb in 1738 and his fairly inaccurate plan of what he called tomb "G"[1] is easy to recognize because of the two large consecutive burial chambers. In 1799 the scientists of the Napoleonic Expedition under the supervision of Edmé François Jomard created a far more accurate plan and correctly reproduced the layout of the tomb for the first time.[2] They labeled it the fifth tomb in the Valley of the Kings and named it "la catacombe de la métempsycose" ("Tomb of the Metempsychosis/transmigration of souls")[3] to distinguish it from the other important tombs in the royal valley. However, they were not able to read the name of the tomb owner Tausret because the hieroglyphs had not yet been deciphered.

Actual scientific investigation of Tausret's rock-cut tomb was begun in the year 1829 by the Franco-Tuscan expedition working in the Valley of the Kings under Jean François Champollion and Ippolito Rosellini. The members of this expedition recorded from some of the scenes the tomb, which they labeled "Tomb no. 9." The results were published in two parallel publications. The first publication by I. Rosellini comprised three volumes of plates that were published as "I monumenti dell' Egitto e della Nubia," vol. I–III (Pisa, 1832–1844). Jean François Champollion's parallel publication with largely the same material and numerous duplicates was published posthumously after his death in 1832 by his older brother Jean Jacques Champollion-Figeac in four volumes as "Monuments de l'Egypte et de la Nubie"(Paris, 1835–1845). The "Notices descriptives" in the supplement of Champollion's "Monuments de l'Egypte" are of great scientific importance as they deal extensively with the tomb's hieroglyphic inscriptions.[4]

A fundamental scientific advancement in regard to the reliefs and inscriptions in the tomb was made by the Prussian expedition led by Karl Richard Lepsius. While spending the winter of 1844/45 in the Valley of the Kings, the expedition recorded key scenes in what they called "Tomb no. 14," which were published shortly afterward.[5] A volume of inscriptions was published in 1900 and supplements the important compendia of plates.

In 1958 Alan H. Gardiner prepared the ground for the subsequent work in the tomb of Tausret by developing a coherent picture of the history of the tomb.[6] One of Gardiner's greatest achievements was being the first to recognize that Tausret was the "Great Royal Wife" of Sety II and not, as had been believed since Champollion, the wife of Siptah. He also assumed correctly that Siptah's images in the tomb demonstrate that the tomb was constructed during his reign, although we now know that work actually commenced even earlier during Sety II's rule. Gardiner recognized that Tausret ascended the throne after Siptah's death and claimed Siptah's regnal years, counting her regnal years from the death of Sety II. This is reflected in the tomb decoration, the image of Siptah being replaced with that of Tausret's deceased husband Sety II. Gardiner further assumed that after the death of Tausret, her reign and that of Siptah were discredited and Siptah and Tausret were regarded as illegitimate rulers. This was one of the reasons the images of Siptah and Tausret are missing in the statue procession of the Min-Festival of Medinet Habu, in which the statues of the kings of the 19th Dynasty are listed in chronological order.[7] Gardiner believed that Tausret's tomb was usurped and expanded during Sethnakht's reign; however, there is no evidence for this.

In recent times, further archaeological investigations have been undertaken in the queen's tomb; the Theban Mapping Project (1997–2008) led by Kent Weeks is especially commendable.[8] An epigraphic survey of all of the texts and inscriptions conducted by the Archaeological Institute of the University of Hamburg (with fieldwork conducted 1983–1989) is nearing completion.[9] Some of the results of this latter survey will be presented in this chapter.

The Construction History of the Tomb

Through fortunate circumstances, we know when construction started on the rock-cut tomb of Queen Tausret, as the date is attested on an ostracon from Thebes (Ostracon Cairo J 72452).[10] The ostracon begins with the words: "Year 2; first month of Winter, day 8, the day when the agent [...] came with [a] dispatch to [the Vizier?] saying 'Start upon the tomb of the King's Great Wife Twosre.'"[11] The ruler is not named, but there is a very detailed list of workmen from this time; by studying this list, researchers have been able to determine that the date refers to the construction of the tomb in the second regnal year of Sety II.[12] This fits well with knowledge that the tomb of Tausret was under construction when the burial of Sety II took place seventy days after his death in the first regnal year of Siptah in "Year 1; third month of Winter, day 11," as attested by a graffito[13] over the entrance of the tomb of Tausret that was inscribed by the Theban workmen shortly after Siptah's ascension to the throne.

Nevertheless, the principal parts of the tomb (Figure 4.1) were built under the rule of Siptah. The structure of the tomb follows the usual plan of the royal tombs common from the mid-19th Dynasty onward. Because of the tomb's straight axis, it can be compared to the tombs of Merenptah (KV 8), Siptah (KV 47), and Ramesses III (KV 11) in the Valley of the Kings.

The main part of the tomb—some 60 meters long—comprises chambers A to J and corresponds to the type and sequence of rooms in a regular royal tomb.[14] An upper and lower group of rooms, both connected by a descending ramp, can be discerned. Both sections are of approximately the same size and structure. The upper part of the tomb consists of the entrance and three corridors (A, B, and C) as well as chambers D and E. The lower part displays a similar sequence of corridors (F and H) and chambers (G, I, and burial chamber J).

A comparison with the royal tombs of that era shows that the tomb of Tausret deviates from the standard in several aspects, however. The dimensions of the main part (A to J) were reduced, making it smaller than the typical king's tomb. Behind the burial chamber (J) are more rooms (K to L), which make the tomb 52 meters longer than the royal tombs used here for comparison. The scientists of the Bonaparte Expedition recognized that there was a second part of the tomb with a burial chamber (L),[15] and both R. Lepsius and A. H. Gardiner believed that there were two burial chambers, one for Tausret and the second for her successor Sethnakht.[16]

The assumption that the second burial chamber was built by Sethnakht has not been confirmed by the most recent investigations, and today there is no doubt that the chambers K to L were built for Tausret herself. Here, hidden under a layer of plaster, in the inner part of the tomb, were the cartouches of Tausret dating to the time of her sole rule.[17] Her titles and names are "Mistress of the Two Lands Satre Meritamun, mistress of the crowns Tausret Setepenmut."[18] The second burial chamber L and the preceding corridors

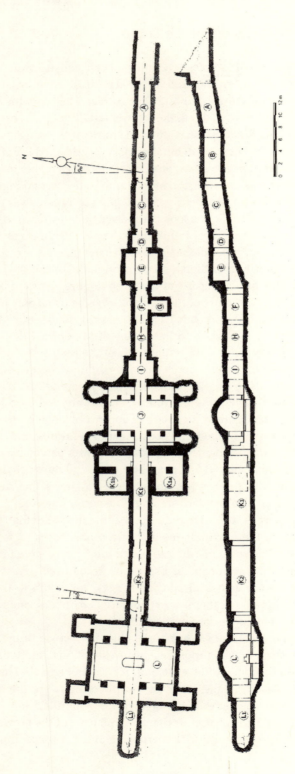

FIGURE 4.1 Plan and section of KV14, the tomb of Tausret and Sethnakht.

K1 and K2 were, like chambers A to J, all designated for Tausret and date to the time of her sole rule.

But this construction phase has, as we will see, its own background. Even before constructing the new section of the tomb with corridors K1, K2, and room L, Tausret had attempted to build a larger burial chamber, but the project failed. The mysterious side chambers K1a and K1b adjoining corridor K1 document this first attempt to construct a monumental royal burial hall.[19] Some significant remains of this chamber, the basic measurements of which are based on the royal cubit, are still preserved. To the east, a row of pillars was planned; the southern pillar still stands in K1a. The single pillar in the northern chamber K1b is also still visible and was subsequently connected to the northern wall of K1b by a brick-built projection.

A crack in the ceiling apparently was the cause for abandoning the work. Two graffiti, one giving the date of regnal year 6, month 2 of the Akhet season, [day] 18, of an unknown king and the other generally naming year 6, month 2 of an indeterminate season, led to the conclusion that construction in K1a/K1b was abandoned in regnal year 6 of Siptah/Tausret.[20] Since it seems that the chamber termed K1a/K1b was supposed to be a burial chamber for a pharaoh, one may assume that already in year 6 of the rule of Siptah/Tausret, before burial chamber K1a/K1b was built, the balance of power at the royal court had shifted in favor of Tausret.[21]

No matter how the date in the incomplete burial chamber is to be interpreted, it is certain that all three successive burial chambers J, K1a/K1b, and L were planned for one and the same royal person, namely Tausret. The unusual number of three burial chambers, including the one (in K1a/K1b) which had to be abandoned, can only be explained by Queen Tausret's rise from king's wife of Sety II to sole ruling pharaoh. Thus the front network of rooms can be associated with the "Great Royal Wife" of Sety II, and the rear part of the tomb with the queen who had risen to pharaoh. The expansion aspired to make the tomb into a funerary monument of royal proportions, which also had its effect on the tomb façade. The height of the façade was increased from its original 2.82 meters (9.18 feet) to 3.32 meters (10.82 feet), and the width was broadened from 2.20 meters (7.21 feet) to 3.15 meters (11.48 feet).

After the death of Sethnakht (c. 1184 BCE), his son Ramesses III decided to use the tomb for his deceased father. No great architectural changes or expansions were performed during Ramesses' reign. The only verified change from the time of Ramesses III is the widening of the doorways from 1.53 meters (5.02 feet) to 1.71 meters (5.6 feet) so that the royal sarcophagus could be brought into the tomb.[22] Cutting back the doorways allowed Sethnakht's 1.62 meter (5.25 feet) wide sarcophagus to be brought in;[23] it was set up in burial chamber L.[24] There is probably a different reason for the holes that were cut into the decorated walls, opposite each other, in the entryway and four of the corridors[25] of the tomb immediately before areas of descent. Beams were mounted in these holes around which the pull ropes were attached to control the descent of a sarcophagus weighing several tons. It is possible that as part of the preparations for Sethnakht's burial, the royal sarcophagus designated for the sole ruler Tausret was removed from the tomb at this time.[26] Interestingly, the doorways that had been cut back to allow the sarcophagus of Sethnakht to be brought in were not returned to their original state, and the beam holes that served for the evacuation of the royal sarcophagus of Tausret were not closed.[27]

Thus, the history of the tomb's construction gives evidence of two building phases: the first phase, in which the type and succession of rooms follows those of a royal tomb, but in smaller dimensions; and a second phase with royal-sized chambers (K1 to L). In the past, the explanation for these findings was that the first building phase of the tomb was constructed for Tausret and the second phase for Sethnakht. It has turned out that this assumption is incorrect. The discovery of the royal cartouches of Tausret at the entry of burial chamber L has ascertained that the entire monument was built for Tausret. The smaller front section of the tomb can be associated with Tausret in her role as royal wife of Sety II and the larger rear section with Tausret as pharaoh. So it is clear that Sethnakht played no role in building the tomb. Ramesses III appropriated Tausret's completed and decorated tomb for the burial of his father Sethnakht and rushed to redecorate it in the seventy days between that king's death and burial.

The Decoration of the Tomb

Study of the decoration of Tausret's tomb has revealed a number of fascinating insights into the tomb's history and the manner in which the queen was depicted. All of the rooms in the tomb—except for the unfinished burial chamber K1a/K1b and the side rooms of burial chambers J and L—are plastered and prepared for a relief decoration. However, only the main part (A to J) of the tomb of the "Great Royal Wife" Tausret was painted. The reliefs of the second building phase (K to L) dating to the time of her sole rule are unpainted because of an apparent shortage of time. Many of the plastered parts of the tomb remained undecorated or had only (preliminary) ink sketches.

On the one hand, the decoration of Tausret's monument follows that of a royal tomb—which is to be expected because of the tomb's location in the Valley of the Kings—and on the other hand, it follows that of a typical queen's tomb of the 19th Dynasty. Just as the various construction phases reflect the changing status of Tausret from "Great Royal Wife" under Sety II to sole ruler of Egypt, so each change in status is reproduced in the images of Tausret. The older images of the queen were plastered over and new images and inscriptions were placed on to the new plaster each time her status changed. Each layer shows a slightly different image of the queen and a new name. However, not every chamber was affected by these changes; with a few exceptions, some rooms, especially the corridors and chambers F to I in the lower part of the tomb, were not touched by the remodeling.

The tomb went through a fundamental change when Ramesses III buried his father, Sethnakht, in KV 14.[28] When Ramesses appropriated the tomb, which was completely decorated for Tausret, he had to replace her images and names with those of his father, which required the following steps. Work started in the first chamber of the tomb (A) where the images of Tausret were replaced by reliefs of Sethnakht. Due to time constraints, starting from corridor B, only a text band with the throne and birth name of Sethnakht, and not his own image, was placed over the replastered images of the previous tomb owner. In corridor B the text band was in relief; from corridor C on it was applied with wide brush

The Versions of the Queen's Images

Most of Tausret's images in her tomb show signs of reworking. The plastered walls reveal three versions of her image; a fourth version is that of Sethnakht.

In the upper chambers, and in corridor A, all four versions can be distinguished. The rooms in the lower part of the tomb were spared any extensive modifications. The texts and images in chambers F to I only display the first version of the "Great Royal Wife" of Sety II as well as the fourth version for Sethnakht.

The queen's image seems to have been repeatedly altered to bring it up to date and adapt it to her new *status quo*. The modifications of the queen's image proceeded from the outside to the inside of the tomb, but because of time pressure her image was not changed in all of the tomb's chambers.

The following table shows the specific locations of the various versions:

	Tausret as Great royal wife	Tausret as regent	Tausret as pharaoh	Sethnakht
Tomb façade	(1)	(?)	([3])	(4)
Chamber A	(1)	(2)	(3)	(4)
Chambers B to E	(1)	—	(3)	(4)
Chambers F to I	(1)	—	—	(4)
Burial chamber J	—	(2)	(3)	(4)
Chambers K1 to burial chamber L	—	—	(3)	(4)

strokes in black ink. The pillars in burial chamber J are a special case: a preliminary drawing of the figure of the king was sketched onto them.

In another step, the old cartouches of Tausret were replaced with those of Sethnakht. The work here was unsystematic, again probably due to time constraints. More than once, the titles preceding the cartouches were ignored, and thus the old royal titles of Tausret were left in front of the names of Sethnakht. The images of kings Siptah and Sety II received special treatment, but wherever it was deemed necessary, the names were changed.

The Sequence of Images of Tausret

The sequence of depictions in the successive plaster layers in scene A-S/1 in the queen's tomb (Figure 4.2) is: First Tausret depicted as queen, next as sole ruler, finally, the superimposed image of Sethnakht.

The image of the first version shows the queen offering to the sun god Re-Horakhty. The queen is wearing the flower/floral crown over the tripartite wig and the vulture cap. She is dressed in a long gown and is holding in each hand a jar, with which she is offering wine to the god.

In the later version Tausret is wearing the blue crown of the pharaoh. Her left arm is crossed in front of her chest, while holding the flail; a lotus flower is in her right hand.

The last image shows Sethnakht, at smaller scale than the earlier images of Tausret, dressed in a long gown, with his right hand raised to the sun god.

FIGURE 4.2 Sequence of depictions in the successive plaster layer in scene A-S/1 in the queen's tomb: first Tausret as Regent, next as sole ruler, and finally, the superimposed image of Sethnakht.

The Decoration of the First Corridor (A)

The wall decoration of the first corridor (A) comprises scenes of the gods (Figures 4.3, 4.4). The gods of the necropolis are depicted as they greet the queen while she is entering the tomb; in return for her offering, they confer on her a "seat in the necropolis." In two scenes, the ruling king Siptah is depicted (A-S/3 and A-N/2).[29] His image was prominently located but was later replaced by that of Sety II. Tausret's political legitimation through Siptah is replaced by "familial" legitimation, which resulted from her role as Sety II's "Great Royal Wife."

The scenes on the southern wall of the first corridor are introduced by a picture that shows the queen offering wine to the falcon-headed god Re-Horakhty (A-S/1). It is a typical representation of royal tombs (as it stresses the relationship of the deceased monarch with the all-important solar deity) and can be found in most of the royal tombs of the 19th and 20th Dynasties. Next, the queen is depicted offering to Anubis (A-S/2), king Siptah is offering to Isis (A-S/3), and in the fourth scene, the queen is shown offering to Horus, son of Isis (A-S/4), followed by her offering to Nefertem (A-S/5)—all deities connected with the afterlife.

On the opposite north wall, other afterlife-associated gods are depicted. To the right, the queen is shown offering to deities Ptah and Maat (A-N/1), followed by Siptah and Tausret before Geb (A-N/2). In the final scene on the left, the queen is depicted offering wine to the ram-headed Re-Horakhty (the evening and nocturnal form of the sun god), behind whom Hathor and Nephthys stand (A-N/3).

The Representation of the Queen in the First Corridor (A)

Most of the images of Queen Tausret in the first corridor were reworked—signaling, as already mentioned, a change in her status. The alterations were performed in the plaster on the face of the corridor walls and are evident in the overlapping reliefs and where material has been removed from the reliefs that are cut into the plaster. It is difficult to determine the individual versions of the various layers because the state of preservation varies in different areas. One is confronted with a confusing array of lines that have to be sorted and arranged into coherent pictures. The titles and names as well as the crowns and stances of the queen are the sole reference points. The difficulty lies in determining the titles and names, crowns and stances of each version and in correlating them.

In the lowest layer, which must be the original version, the queen is depicted with either the vulture cap, the double feathers crown, or the so-called floral crown and can be identified by an inscription as "Great Royal Wife" of Sety II. On a middle layer, which was only painted and is barely preserved, the names

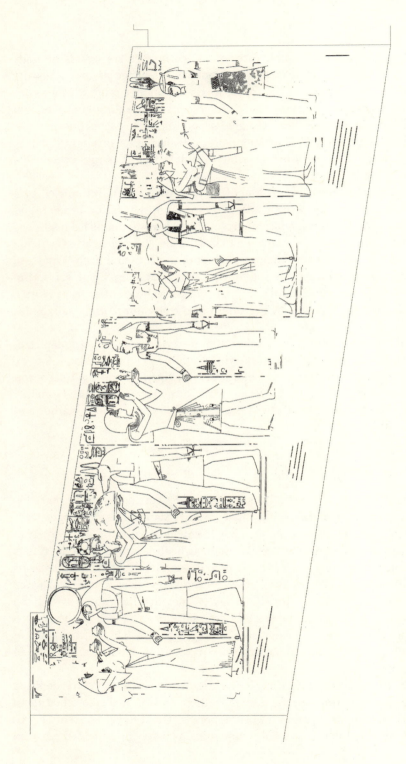

FIGURE 4.3 The wall decoration of the first corridor (A) of the tomb of Tausret comprises scenes of the gods as they greet the queen. The south wall.

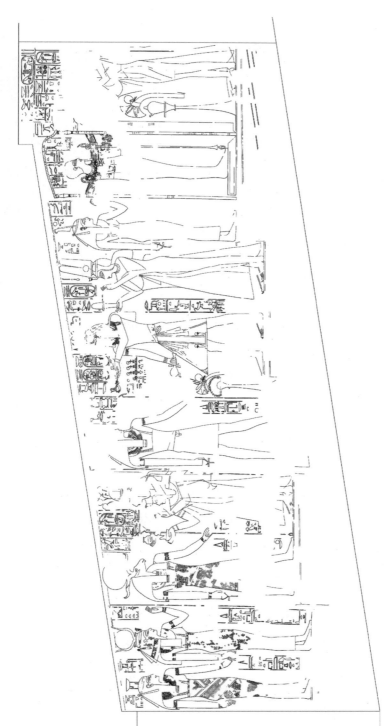

FIGURE 4.4 The wall decoration of the first corridor (A) of the tomb of Tausret comprises scenes of the gods as they greet the queen. The north wall.

of the queen are written in two cartouches. They do not contain the queen's names dating to the time of her sole rule but from the time of her co-regency.[30] In a superimposed third layer, Tausret is represented as pharaoh with the blue crown. The topmost layer, which lies over the third layer, depicts Sethnakht.

Different versions can also be distinguished for the queen's regalia and stance; one version shows the queen with the flail before a god, and another depicts the queen offering to a god. The main problem lies in assigning the various crowns to the appropriate stance of the queen. Which version belongs to which queen with which crown?

In previous publications, I identified images of the queen with the flail as the "Great Royal Wife,"[31] because the flail is part of the customary regalia of a "Great Royal Wife."[32] Based on this, by process of elimination, the "offering" queen could be associated with the ruling queen. It seemed reasonable that a ruling queen would offer to the gods. A detailed analysis of the scenes in the first corridor has revealed that it is actually the other way around. By comparing the inscriptions and examining the relief cuts, it is possible to demonstrate that the "offering" queen in the tomb of Tausret is adorned with the vulture cap, double feathers crown, or floral crown; the images of the queen holding the flail belong to the depictions of the blue crown and represent the queen of the third phase of decoration. Cuts near the chest and traces of chipping on the upper arm indicate that the "flail" of the ruling queen is superimposed on the arm of the "offering" queen and is thus a later version.

The Representation of the Queen in the First Phase

The first image on the north wall of the first corridor (A-N/1) plays a key role in assigning the "offering" queen to the first phase of the "Great Royal Wife." It shows the queen offering flowers to Ptah and Maat. In the accompanying text, the "offering" queen is identified as "Great Royal Wife":

> An offering of flowers to her father [Ptah] from the [Great] royal wife, mistress of the Two Lands, ruler of Upper and Lower Egypt, mistress of esteem (?), and sweet of love, Tausret, [justified].

Texts associating Tausret with the names of rituals on the lowest layer can also be assigned to the image of the "Great Royal Wife" of the first version.[33] One of the rituals is that of the queen offering wine to the ram-headed Re-Horakhty (A-N/3): "An offering of wine to [her father] Re-Horakhty."

A comparison with the other images of the "offering" queen, especially in chamber I, confirms this relationship. With one exception in the first corridor (A-S/2), which will be dealt with later in the chapter, all of the inscriptions call the "offering" queen "Great Royal Wife." Chamber I, the decoration of which is entirely from the first version and was not redecorated for Tausret as pharaoh in the last phase, always displays the image of the "offering" queen.[34] Although the original scenes are covered by a layer of plaster for the later images of Sethnakht, it is possible to determine them through the preserved inscriptions.

The Representation of the Queen in the Second Phase

The second scene on the south wall of the first corridor (Sc. A-S/2) shows an offering to Anubis that seems to stand in contradiction to what was said earlier.[35] In one of the texts to this scene (which is not a relief, but a painting, and which was composed to accompany the image of the "offering" queen), the name of Queen Tausret was written in two cartouches. In comparison to the first version, which includes a short form of the name of the "Great Royal Wife" in sunk relief,[36] the text to this scene, with painted hieroglyphs, associates the "offering" queen from the first version with a name written in two cartouches. The text reads:

> Bringing of the offering to her father Anubis, who is in his wrappings, by the mistress of the Two Lands [Satre] Henut Ta[meri], mistress of the crowns Tausret, [beneficial to] Mut.[37]

The names listed in the inscription differ from the known names of the sole ruler Satre Meritamun Tausret Setepetenmut; so the names in this scene would seem to refer to Tausret as regent. The name of the regent can be ascertained because in this version the throne name is cut by the later blue crown of the third version and thus cannot belong to the third version.

The Representation of the Queen in the Third Phase

We can identify the image of the ruling queen in the third phase with certainty, although this image is also severely damaged due to its exposed position. In this version, the queen is depicted with the blue crown of a ruling pharaoh. She is holding the flail in her fist in front of her chest, while her other hand is hanging down at the side of her body and is holding a lotus flower or a piece of cloth.[38]

This third version is the most frequent representation of Tausret. It can be found in the first corridor of the tomb (A), as well as in corridors B, C, and E in the scenes from Chapter 145 of the Book of the Dead. Under angled light it is possible to see the image of the queen as pharaoh under the plaster on the pillars in burial chamber J, which later were decorated with the image of Sethnakht (Ad, Ba, Ca, Db, Ga). This final version is missing only in chambers F, H, and I, in which none of the images of the queen were changed and all of the titles and cartouches of the "Great Royal Wife" are preserved.

The Representation of the King in the First Corridor (A)

The images of the king in the first corridor were treated differently. While all of the images of the queen in the first corridor were completely reworked, the images of the king on the southern and northern wall (A-S/3; A-N/2) were not touched. Only the cartouches were changed. J. F. Champollion and R. Lepsius noted that the throne and birth names of Sety II, "Lord of the Two Lands Userkheperurere Merire Meriamun and Lord of appearances Seti Merenptah," were superimposed on the older cartouches of Siptah, "Lord of the Two lands Akhenre Setepenre and Lord of appearances Merenptah Siptah."[39] The names of Sethnakht do not appear.

It was believed that the change of names from Siptah to Sety II meant that Siptah was Tausret's first royal husband and Sety II married Tausret after Siptah's death. Based on external documents, A. H. Gardiner was able to demonstrate that from the beginning Tausret had been married to Sety II and had never been Siptah's wife. He also discovered that Siptah had not ruled before Sety II, but was his successor.[40] The simplest and most convincing explanation for the name change from Siptah to Sety II in the tomb of Tausret is Gardiner's assumption that Siptah was depicted in the tomb because the tomb was decorated during his reign.[41] By including the king in the decoration, Tausret was legitimizing the construction of her tomb in the Valley of the Kings in Thebes. When Siptah died, her deceased husband Sety II assumed the role of legitimization posthumously.

The Representation of Sethnakht from the Time of the Tomb's Usurpation

Ramesses III made the last changes to the queen's tomb after the death of Sethnakht. Although Sethnakht already had his own well-advanced tomb (KV 11) in the Valley of the Kings, Tausret's tomb was selected for his burial. When the tomb was rededicated to Sethnakht, all of Tausret's images in corridor A were covered over and a smaller-sized image of Sethnakht was superimposed. The images of Sethnakht only reached up to the queen's shoulders and were thus much smaller than those of the queen, which they concealed.

Summarizing Remarks

Assessing the representational evidence in the first corridor shows that the modifications that can be detected are linked to changes in the queen's status. Each version reflects Tausret's new status and utilizes a new and differentiated image of the queen. The changes to the decoration cover the time until Sethnakht's burial and can be summarized as follows.

Phase 1: Tausret as "Great Royal Wife"

In the first decoration phase of corridor A, Tausret is the "Great Royal Wife" of Sety II. She is adorned with the usual crowns of the queens and is depicted offering to the gods. Siptah's presence legitimizes her as owner of a tomb in the Valley of the Kings.

Phase 2: Tausret as Regent

Tausret depicts herself as regent on a par with Siptah. Her new status is documented in the extended version of her royal name in two cartouches within the names of the rituals.

Phase 3: Tausret as Pharaoh

Although Tausret is sole ruler, she derives her role as pharaoh from her position as former "Great Royal Wife" of Sety II. She holds the flail of the "Great Royal Wife" in the one hand and the lotus flower or piece of cloth in the other; at the same time she demonstrates her power as pharaoh by wearing the blue crown of a ruler.

Phase 4: Redecorating the Tomb for Sethnakht

Ramesses III ordered the burial of Sethnakht in the tomb of Tausret. All of Tausret's images are covered up with a layer of plaster and are replaced by those of Sethnakht in corridor A, while Sety II's images and names are preserved. With the rededication of Tausret's images and inscriptions to Sethnakht, the decoration of the tomb focuses entirely on Sethnakht.

The Themes of the Texts and Images in the Tomb

The texts and images in the tomb encompass various themes. In the upper rooms, Tausret's journey to the realm of Osiris is depicted (corridor B and C, chamber E), followed by scenes relating to the embalmment (D and G) and the Opening of the Mouth ritual necessary for resurrection (F and H), as well as the divine tribunal (I). Both of the burial chambers (J and L) and the connecting corridors (K1, K2) are decorated with scenes from the sun god's journey through the netherworld, which Tausret enters upon her death as a female pharaoh (burial chamber J and L, corridors K1 and K2).

Tausret's Journey to the Realm of Osiris

The decoration of corridors B and C and of chamber E resumes the topics that are addressed in the entryway corridor (A). Tausret is greeted by the gods of the netherworld who promise her a place in the necropolis. Her entry and her journey through the divisions of the netherworld are the theme of the wall reliefs

in corridors B and C and in chamber E. The texts from Chapter 145 of the
Book of the Dead from the New Kingdom describe the difficult journey of the
"Great Royal Wife" to the realm of Osiris, a journey during which the queen
is accompanied by her husband Sety II. In comparison to the royal tombs of
the Ramesside Period, which address in the entry corridors the netherworld
journey of the sun god and where the deceased king in the role of a sun priest
professes to know the movements of the sun god, Chapter 145 of the Book of
the Dead deals with the journey the queen has to take on her way to the realm
of Osiris.

This chapter lists eighteen gates of the netherworld in Tausret's tomb. Each
gate is depicted as a register-filling monument with knife-wielding guards.
The arrangement of the representations is always the same. On one side of the
gate stands the guard, on the other the queen; between the gate and the queen
vertical lines of text list the specific spell that needs to be recited. The texts
give the necessary information so that the deceased queen can pass through
the gates. She has to know the names of the gates and individual guards; she
needs to be purified with a certain type of water, anointed with a certain type of
salve, dressed in a certain gown, and equipped with a certain staff.

At the end of her journey, the queen reaches the Hall of Osiris in room E.
There Horus and Anubis receive the queen and accompany her to the god of
the dead, Osiris, who decides whether she can enter his realm. The image of
the god standing in a shrine is of fundamental importance and is placed above
the descent into the lower part of the tomb. It signals the deceased queen's
admission into the realm of Osiris.

While the queen is passing through the gates, she is accompanied by her
husband Sety II, whose image appears at three of the gates of the netherworld:
in corridor B in front of the first and second gate (B-S/1 and B-N/1) and in
room E in front of the sixteenth gate (E-N/2). The three images of Sety II were
replaced by those of Sethnakht during the last phase of decorating the tomb by
superimposing the names of Sethnakht over the cartouches of Sety II.[42]

The images of the queen also show signs of modifications, which hardly
differ from those in entry corridor A. The first and third version of Tausret, as
well as the last version for Sethnakht can be identified. The bottom layer displays the images of the first version. The queen is represented with her arms
raised in adoration. Her arms are adorned with bracelets and reach into the
block of text next to the gate. She is wearing a long gown and the vulture cap,
floral crown, or double feathers crown.

The image in the third version shows Tausret with the blue crown. As with
her image in corridor A, she is holding a flail in her raised hand and a lotus
flower in the lowered hand. The changes also affected the title and names of the
queen, which are now connected with two cartouches.

Within the texts of Chapter 145 of the Book of the Dead, the names of the
"Great Royal Wife" from the first version are written in only one cartouche.

In the version of the regnant queen, there are two cartouches with the throne and birth names. To steer clear of any difficulties associated with an incomplete name, in chambers C and E, and probably also in B (where checking the cartouches is impossible because of the level of destruction), on one wall the throne name of the ruler, introduced by the title "Lord of the Two Lands" was placed, and on the other wall the birth name, preceded by the ruler's title "lord of appearances."

The rededication to Sethnakht evidently proceeded very quickly. The images of the queen were completely plastered over and the names of Sethnakht added to this new surface; in corridor B his names are in relief and in the later rooms in black ink. Due to the haste, some of the names in the cartouches of Sethnakht are misspelled.[43]

Embalmment, Opening of the Mouth, and Judgment of the Dead (Chambers D, G, and I)

The Gods of Embalming in Chambers D and G

Chamber D lies between corridor C and chamber E. On the walls of the chamber, the gods of embalming are depicted, which is not unusual in a so-called well room of the royal prototype of the early 19th Dynasty.

The proper embalming room, however, was chamber G in the lower part of the tomb. There the mummy of the deceased is shown laid out on a bier. The jackal-headed Anubis, who is in charge of embalming, is bent over the mummy. After the physical restitution of the "Great Royal Wife," she offers to the gods of the embalming place. The offering is received by, on the east wall, Imseti, Anubis in his wrappings, Duamutef, Isis, and [Neith], and on the opposite west wall by Hapi, Anubis in front of the hall of gods, Qebehsenuef, [Nephthys], and [Selket].

The Opening of the Mouth Ritual in Chambers F-H[44]

Behind the ramp descending into the lower part of the tomb are two corridors, which contain an outline of the ceremony of the Opening of the Mouth. The ritual texts are distributed in Tausret's tomb on the walls of chambers F and H in such a manner that scenes 1–12 appear in corridor (F) and scenes 13–26 in the fifth corridor (H) of the tomb. The sequence of scenes begins in the fourth and fifth corridors on the left wall and jumps, at the end of the wall, onto the right wall in the same direction of writing. Because of this peculiarity, the priests depicted on the left wall are looking, as usual, into the tomb, while those on the right wall are looking out of the tomb, which is unusual.

Interestingly, the statue of the queen that should be reanimated during the Opening of the Mouth ritual is never depicted as a queen with the blue crown and flail. She always appears as "Great Royal Wife," with the double feathers crown or the so-called floral crown, which are typical for the image of the queen as depicted in the first phase. The statue was not modified into a statue of the regnant queen. The ritual texts were not altered either. There are only three places in the passage to chamber G in which the title of the ruling queen was minimally adapted, but nowhere else.[45]

All of the images and cartouches of the "Great Royal Wife" of Sety II were covered by plaster dating to Ramesses III, on which the cartouches of Sethnakht are displayed. The double feathers crown (scene 1, 2) or the floral crown (scene 6) from the first phase can be partially identified. Only the image in the northeast corner of corridor F was not plastered over; it shows the queen with the double feathers crown—according to the ritual—in the stance and attire of the god Amun.

The Gods of the Judgment Hall of Osiris in Chamber I

Following the chambers with the scenes from the Opening of the Mouth ritual is a chamber in which Tausret is depicted offering to various gods.[46] The room takes up the subject matter of the scenes of the deities in entryway corridor A. All of the representations are from the first phase of the tomb's decoration. The image of the queen was not altered.

The deities, to whom the queen is offering, can be identified as gods of the judgment hall of Osiris. Comparison of this room with the "hall of the divine tribunal" is thus probable, especially since in the royal tombs of the 19th Dynasty the texts and images in this room relate to the judgment of the dead.[47] Presiding over the court, on the entry wall, is Osiris, enthroned in his shrine and flanked by Isis and Nephthys. On the opposite south wall are Re-Horakhty and Maat as members of the tribunal, as well as Thoth with his writing palette who is delivering the judgment on the deceased (Figure 4.5, see insert).

The Netherworld of the Sun God in Burial Chambers J and L and the Connecting Corridors (K1, K2)[48]

Burial Chamber J

Although the proportions of the architecture are reduced for the king's wife, burial chamber J was decorated according to the standards of a king's tomb. The decoration is almost identical to that of burial chamber L, which was constructed for Tausret during her sole rule. There are some parallels to the decoration of the burial chambers of Merenptah (KV 8) and Ramesses III (KV 11).

The chamber is divided into various sections: a middle part, which has a barrel vault ceiling; an east and west wing, which border like an elevated podium the sunken lower middle part on the east and west side; and two rows, of four pillars each, which flank the middle part of the chamber on its east and west sides and at the same time support the barrel vault. The pillars are decorated with images of gods and the king, the walls with scenes from the night journey of the sun god through the netherworld. In the tunnel vault that is 5.31 meters (17.42 feet) high is an astronomical ceiling with images of the star constellations and decans.

The south wall of the hall shows part of the "Book of the Earth," which deals with the resurrection of the sun god at the end of the night and his reanimation. The dead figure of the sun god is symbolized in the upper register as a supine mummy surrounded by discs and stars, the reanimation below by the standing mummy, which is surrounded by various beings.

On the north wall is a monumental depiction of the final scene of the "Book of Caverns" (Figure 4.6, see insert). Above the image of a ram-headed, winged being, symbolizing the netherworldly sun god, the resurrection of the sun is thematized in a fashion typical of the final scenes of the afterlife books. There are three manifestations of the sun god: as the sun disk, as the child, and finally as the scarab who is pushing the sun disk in front of him. Two pairs of arms are depicted reaching forth from the ceiling to welcome the trinity of the sun's manifestations.

On the east wall, in front of the row of pillars, are excerpts from the "Book of Gates." The texts can be divided into a first and second version. The texts of the first version date to the time of the regency and can be identified as preliminary ink sketches on the south and north side of the elevated east wing. They are partially covered by painted relief of the second version, probably dating to the time of Tausret's sole rule. On the southern wall of the east wing is a preliminary sketch of the regent's name "Osiris King Satre Henut Tameri" which belongs to the first version of the decoration of the sarcophagus hall. The same name is preserved in the first corridor of the tomb (A-S/2) where it belongs to the second phase of decoration.

The late date of the decoration in burial chamber J is confirmed by the frieze on the walls of the sunken middle part—in which seventy-seven objects of the royal funerary equipment are listed. There are two thrones among the illustrated grave goods, which display the sign of unification of the Two Lands. Because of the doubling of the throne, it is debatable if the frieze belongs to the time of Tausret's and Siptah's regency or the time of her sole rule, during which Tausret legitimized her rule with her association with Sety II, whose image has been preserved on a pillar (J-F/b) in burial chamber J.

Although the mummy of Tausret has not been found, luckily the queen's sarcophagus, which was once set up in the burial chamber, has been preserved. It was found in the present writer's excavation of the neighboring tomb of Bay (KV 13), where it was reworked for a son of Ramesses III and reused.[49]

The Sarcophagus of Queen Tausret

The sarcophagus of Queen Tausret (length 2.88 meters/9.18 feet; width 1.10 meters/3.6 feet; height 1.10 + 0.53 meters/3.6 + 1.73 feet) was found reused in the neighboring tomb of Bay (KV 13). The lid and the basin were redecorated under Ramesses III for prince Amunherkhopeshef; the essential elements of the original decoration were preserved (Figure 4.7A and 4.7B).

The modifications of the lid affected the sculpted mummiform figure of the queen; her long tripartite wig with the vulture cap was changed into a globular hairstyle with the curls of a prince. The queen's title remained; her name was scratched out and was replaced almost everywhere with the name of Amunherkhopeshef.

The sculpted mummiform figure of the queen is surrounded by a Mehen-serpent (uroboros). Beneath her crossed arms, a line of texts begins with an utterance of the goddess of the sky Nut. To the right and left in five transverse lines are the utterances of the gods, who are protecting the queen.

The transverse lines form the frame of the image fields. At the very top, flanking the head, is the winged, ram-headed figure of the nocturnal sun god, holding standards in his talons. In the second field is the representation of Anubis, and in the third those of the gods of the canopic jars, Duamutef and Neith to the left of Imseti, Qebehsenuef and Selket to the right of Hapi. In the fourth field, the queen is shown praying to Sokar-Osiris on the left and to Osiris on the right. When the sarcophagus lid was usurped, the figures of the queen were removed and replaced by an image of a mummiform son of Horus.

The field at the foot of the sarcophagus shows the gods facing the tip of the foot. To the left is the goddess of the east and to the right the goddess of the west, both in a gesture of greeting in front of the name of the "Great royal wife, lord/mistress of the Two Lands [Tausret]." In both pendentives an eye of Horus has been placed to avoid a blank space.

A similar segmentation of the sarcophagus lid can be found earlier on the sarcophagus of Merenptah and later on the coffins of the Third Intermediate Period. The decoration of Tausret's sarcophagus lid is thus an important link between the early and late coffins.

The sarcophagus of Tausret from the time of her sole rule may be the sarcophagus that was found together with the queen's sarcophagus in the tomb of Bay (KV 13) (length 3.20 meters/10.49 feet; width 1.45 meters/4.75 feet; height 1.40 + 0.80 meters/4.59 + 2.62 feet). The sketched decoration on this sarcophagus is similar to the decoration of the smaller queen's sarcophagus; however, because of missing inscriptions, it cannot be assigned to pharaoh Tausret with certainty. It remained unfinished, was reworked, and then reused by Ramesses III (?) for the burial of prince Mentuherkhopeshef.

Connecting Corridors K1 and K2

The annex (K1, K2, and burial chamber L), connected to burial chamber J during the first construction phase, can unequivocally be dated to the time of Tausret's sole rule. Her cartouches dating to this time can be found on the reveals in front of burial chamber L.[50]

The walls of both of the connecting corridors (K1 and K2) between the burial chambers (J and L) are decorated with texts from the Amduat, which describe the sixth to ninth hour of the sun god's nocturnal journey through the divisions of the underworld. Despite the fairly late decoration phase, it is

FIGURE 4.7A and B Sarcophagus of Queen Tausret discovered in the tomb of Bay (KV 13).

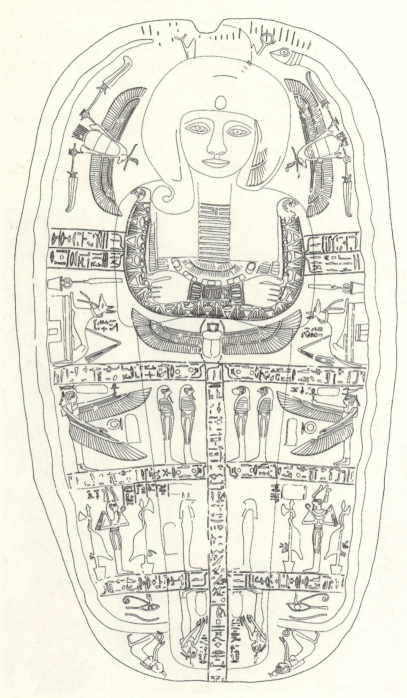

FIGURE 4.7A and B (continued)

possible to distinguish a first and second version, which both trace back to Tausret. Only the second version is in relief; the first version is preserved fragmentarily in the form of a preliminary sketch. The sketch shows that in the first version corridor K1 was initially supposed to be decorated with images and texts of the sixth and seventh hour of the Amduat and then corridor K2 with the eighth and ninth hour of the Amduat. Apparently the plan was to place the subsequent hour-texts on opposite walls. However, this plan was abandoned in the second version and the texts were arranged in a circular distribution around the sides of the walls. First the southern walls were decorated with the sixth hour in K1 and then with the seventh hour in K2, followed by (from left to right) the northern wall of K2 with the eighth and then that of K1 with the ninth hour of the Amduat. In the final version, the sixth and ninth hour in K1 and the seventh and eighth hour of the Amduat in K2 were facing each other on the southern and northern walls.

The effect of the circular distribution of the reliefs was that the sun bark traveled from left to right on the southern wall and on the northern wall, and thus an imaginary "ferry service" of the sun bark was established between burial chambers L and J.

The texts begin with the sixth hour of the Amduat, during which the sun god unites with his body.[51] This hour denotes the beginning of the second half of the night, at the end of which the sun god appears on the eastern horizon. Placing the sixth to ninth hour between the two burial chambers gives the concept of resurrection a deeper meaning.

Burial Chamber L

The architecture of burial chamber L basically replicates the architecture of burial chamber J, but on a larger scale. There are differences between the two chambers, however, especially in the decoration. Although construction was completed, there was not enough time to decorate all of the walls. Only the vaulted ceiling, the east wing of the burial chamber, and the row of pillars of the east wing are decorated. Beneath the tunnel vault which is decorated with an astronomical ceiling now stands Sethnakht's sarcophagus, which was modeled after the royal sarcophagi of the late 19th Dynasty.

The sarcophagus of Sethnakht is probably located where the sarcophagus of Tausret in her role as pharaoh originally stood, and from where it was removed after the usurpation of the tomb to make room for Sethnakht's burial.[52] Perhaps Tausret's kingly sarcophagus is the enormous second sarcophagus from the tomb of Bay (KV 13) that remained unfinished and was later remodeled for prince Mentuherchopeschef.[53] It is thus unknown if Tausret was ever laid to rest in the tomb so extensively prepared for her.

Summary

In its final, preserved version, the tomb of Tausret is a regular king's tomb. Construction was begun at the end of the second year of Sety II; after his death, it was continued by Siptah and was finalized by Tausret as sole ruler. The location of the tomb in the Valley of the Kings demonstrates that the queen had already assumed a very prominent role as the "Great Royal Wife" of Sety II.

One of the special features of the tomb is that the original plan was changed numerous times and that these changes are documented in the construction of the monument. They can be found in all of the important parts of the architecture, decoration, and iconography of the queen.

The changes in the architecture are most evident. The tomb was originally planned as a small version of a king's tomb, but it was enlarged to the dimensions of a real king's tomb by leaps and bounds. This expansion began behind the front burial chamber J.

The new dimensions of the tomb's architecture also influenced the decoration. In the beginning, it contained elements from Ramesside private tombs, including almost the complete Chapter 145 of the Book of the Dead as well as the first scenes of the Opening of the Mouth ritual (scenes 1–27). Suddenly and without a transition, the decorative program was changed to a royal iconographic model, in which the royal books of the netherworld play a central role. The transformation is documented for the first time in the afterlife books in burial chamber J.

Especially evident are the modifications of the queen's image, which record her different degrees of rank. The queen's earlier degrees of rank were replaced with her new ones. This was done by plastering over the obsolete older images throughout most of the tomb. Thus the queen's images display numerous layers. The layer of the "Great Royal Wife," the regent, and sole ruler can all be found in the uppermost corridor of the tomb; the last layer of the sole ruler can only be found in the additions beyond burial chamber J.

The tomb of Tausret is thus the only royal tomb in the Valley of the Kings in which the history of the interred pharaoh can be read from the architecture, the images, and the iconography. In fact, it is the only royal tomb that documents the rise of a member of the royal family to pharaoh.

The appropriation of the tomb for Sethnakht was done for mainly pragmatic reasons. Ramesses III chose this tomb for his father's burial primarily because it fulfilled the requirements of a completed king's tomb better than Sethnakht's own unfinished tomb, KV 11. It is unclear if other reasons played a role in this appropriation, but it is possible that the queen was viewed as having lost her right to a royal tomb and was therefore removed from the Valley of the Kings.

When the tomb was rededicated to Sethnakht, both of Tausret's sarcophagi had to be removed to make room for Sethnakht's sarcophagus. The first sarcophagus of the "Great Royal Wife" of Sety II was relocated into the tomb of Bay (KV 13) by Ramesses III and reused by his son Amunherkopeschef. The same must have happened to her other sarcophagus, which was much larger and dedicated to pharaoh Tausret. It can probably be identified with the enormous second sarcophagus in the tomb of Bay (KV 13), which was left in its still unfinished state and was reused by Ramesses III for his son Mentuherkopeschef.[54]

The appropriation of Tausret's decorated tomb also enabled Ramesses III to directly link the 20th Dynasty to the 19th Dynasty. When the tomb was rededicated to Sethnakht, the image of Sety II remained untouched in crucial places. The king was thus able to place his father Sethnakht in the direct line of succession to Sety II and bypass the time of what were now viewed as the "empty years" connected with Siptah and Tausret[55] at the end of the 19th Dynasty.

5

The "Temple of Millions of Years" of Tausret

RICHARD H. WILKINSON

Like many of her royal predecessors, Pharaoh Tausret constructed not only a tomb to receive her body in the Valley of the Kings in western Thebes, but also a temple nearby to honor and sustain her spirit throughout time. Egyptian pharaohs of the New Kingdom era built such temples—called by the Egyptians "temples of millions of years"[1]—on the flat desert edge between the mountainous ridges that circle the royal valley and the cultivated fields that flanked the Nile. These monuments, often called "mortuary temples" or "memorial temples" in earlier works, were not truly such[2] and often began to function during the lifetimes of the individuals to whom they were dedicated. Yet they were constructed to aid the perpetuation of kings (and occasionally non-royals) and could be considered a part of the afterlife machinery of the pharaohs—the other half, as it were, of the royal burial complex. While earlier kings had constructed pyramids with directly adjoining mortuary temples, New Kingdom monarchs built their "temples of millions of years" at a distance from their tombs. The monuments were constructed adjacent to the cultivated fields and canals connected to the Nile to give them easy access for the delivery of produce and other goods that would be offered to the spirit of the pharaoh during the monarch's lifetime and, theoretically, throughout eternity. All of the New Kingdom's greatest pharaohs constructed such temples; and Pharaoh-Queen Tausret, who was probably the last ruling descendent of Ramesses the Great, made herself a part of this illustrious group.

Over three thousand years ago, on some early morning before the sun's heat became uncomfortable on the desert's edge, Egyptian priests convened at the site that had been chosen for the building of a new temple for Tausret in a space between the monuments of Ramesses the Great and that of his son and successor, Merenptah. Carefully the priests began to enact rituals that were already ancient in their time—rituals that would garner the blessings of the gods for the temple site and for the work of building that lay ahead. Slowly and methodically they moved in procession around the complex network of trenches cut to receive the temple's foundations, scattering small beads and amulets throughout the trenches and pausing occasionally to fill specifically prepared foundation pits with particular offerings at key points in the temple's plan. Next, the first, especially symbolic, foundation stone was perhaps lowered into one of the trenches with an inscription already painted on its upper surface marking the date and significance of the event, or a pre-placed stone was ceremoniously inscribed with the foundation text. In either case, drink offerings—perhaps of costly wine—were probably made at this key point in the ceremony. Doubtless Pharaoh Queen Tausret was present to witness the establishment of her temple which, if completed, would ensure sacrifices for her spirit long after her physical life, and which would link her to history by tying her firmly to the memory of her great ancestor.

Excavating a Lost Temple

The temple of Tausret was, in a sense, doubly lost to history. First, the temple appears to have been demolished at some point after its construction in ancient times and its stone hauled away by one or more pharaohs for their own building projects. But the temple was also "lost" to modern scientific archaeology as a result of William Flinders Petrie's exploration of the site, which was not thorough enough to properly discern the true nature of the temple's past history. Between 2004 and 2011, however, excavations conducted by the University of Arizona Egyptian Expedition have shown that Petrie was perhaps not even present during the time his men cursorily worked on the site and that his published report on the work was often not based on actual excavation. The results of this recent archaeological investigation of the temple site demonstrate this situation in a number of ways, perhaps none more clearly than the glaring differences discovered between Petrie's plan of the temple of Tausret and the actual plan of many of its foundation trenches and surface areas. In the example given here (Figure 5.1), from the southwest quadrant of the site, it can be seen that most of the surface areas (rooms of the temple) as mapped by Petrie or his men (in black lines) are very different from the actual shape and even number of the surfaces revealed by our excavation (light gray lines).

The reason for these—and many other—differences between Petrie's published plan and the reality of the temple remains is apparently a result of temple features as recorded on the earlier plan having been "guessed at" based on the shape and size of the mounds of debris covering the surface in Petrie's time. Whether Petrie's men or Petrie himself produced the plan published in his report, the result was that the actual facts of the temple's design and plan were lost until the recent excavations uncovered them.

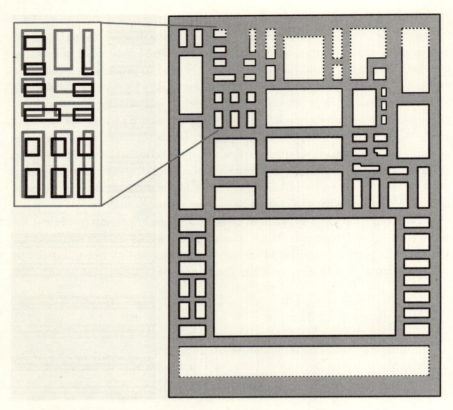

FIGURE 5.1 Plan of the temple of Tausret as mapped by the UAEE. The inset shows one of the sections of the temple mapped incorrectly by Petrie (gray lines) and as it actually was found to be (black lines) when excavated. Graphic by Aaryn S. Brewer.

Some thirty-one hundred years later, on one morning in the year 1896 of the present era, the English archaeologist William Flinders Petrie (Figure 5.2, see insert) walked the surface of Tausret's long vanished and long forgotten temple site and began to instruct his workmen to examine the area. Eventually, when the laborers' work was completed, Petrie briefly described the site and included a plan[3] of its network of foundation trenches in his book *Six Temples at Thebes,* in which he recorded his exploration of a half dozen Theban temples in that same season. Carefully documenting some small finds but noting a lack of major remains and any evidence of building beyond the placement of a few foundation stones, Petrie essentially dismissed the temple. Since that time the site has been virtually ignored on the assumption that the temple was never completed in antiquity.[4]

However, a little over a hundred years later—not much more than a blink of historical time, but a period of great advances in archaeological techniques and possibilities—researchers of the University of Arizona Egyptian Expedition (UAEE)[5] studied Petrie's unpublished notes, pored over satellite imagery of the temple site, and surveyed its barren, undulating surface only to conclude that the temple had never really been excavated and might have been far more developed than Petrie guessed.

In 2004, Egypt's Supreme Council of Antiquities[6] granted the Expedition permission to examine the site (Figure 5.3) and to carefully record and publish any remains that might actually exist of this temple. With the first of what would be eight field seasons[7] of excavation at the site, from 2004 to 2011,[8] the UAEE set out to recover the actual history, nature, and extent of a temple fascinating by virtue of its being conceived for one of Egypt's handful of female pharaohs. In addition, it is the only surviving temple, beyond that of Hatshepsut in nearby Deir el-Bahri, dedicated to a regnant Egyptian queen.

Was the Temple of Tausret Actually Excavated by Petrie?

William Flinders Petrie was a true giant in Egyptian archaeology and we owe much to him. His accomplishments were many, and the list of sites he excavated is amazingly long; but his work was often hurried and sometimes, as a result, it was flawed. This seems to have been the case in Petrie's investigation of the site of the temple of Tausret. It is important to realize this as Petrie's assessment of the temple has sidetracked generations of archaeologists from understanding the site and what it can tell us about Tausret.

In our work on the temple site we immediately began to find evidence that it had not, in fact, been examined to any great degree. Although Petrie stated unequivocally that the temple's foundation trenches were all cleared by his

FIGURE 5.3 Part of the Tausret temple site undergoing initial excavation by the University of Arizona Egyptian Expedition in 2006. Photograph by UAEE.

men,[9] we found that a great many of the trenches and their adjoining surface areas were actually completely undisturbed and showed no evidence of previous excavation. This also could be seen in the presence of foundation blocks (see Figure 5.4) and a multitude of small artifacts in many areas of the site.[10]

Often we found that the site was disturbed only in areas where foundation pits were cut by the Egyptians to receive offerings for the gods. Due to their experience in other temples, Petrie's men knew where to look for these pits and it became clear to us that they had narrowly concentrated their efforts to discover and retrieve the foundation offerings from Tausret's monument. Their motive was also perfectly clear as Petrie specifically mentions that he paid the men handsomely for these finds.[11]

In addition, we have discovered inscriptions that Petrie would certainly have published had he found them—including important foundation texts[12] mentioned in the introduction to this chapter, which were put in place when the monument was begun and which show that Tausret must have reigned longer than we had previously guessed.[13]

On a much larger scale, we have found a number of architectural features on the site that undoubtedly Petrie would have mentioned had he been present during its investigation, and if the site truly had been excavated.[14] Most telling of all, however, we have found Petrie's published plan of the temple to be inaccurate in dozens of areas. In many cases, not only are the size and shape

FIGURE 5.4 Stone blocks and other features of the temple beginning to appear. Photograph by UAEE.

of the temple's foundation trenches and surface areas (the temple's courts and rooms) incorrectly mapped, but also even the number of surfaces in a given area. It is clear that much of the temple plan was in fact merely guessed at-based on the size and shapes of mounds of debris covering the temple site.[15] These facts all suggest that Petrie may often have not been present at the site when it was explored by his workmen and that their exploration may have been far more limited than he realized. Petrie himself was likely elsewhere supervising the excavation of one of the other five temples that he also excavated in the single season of 1896. Thus it seems likely that he may have been told by his men that the Tausret temple site was thoroughly examined when, in fact, it was merely probed in selected, potentially promising areas, and a minimal amount of digging accomplished in other areas to try to establish the plan of the monument.

Recovering the History of the Temple

Whatever the actual nature of Petrie's investigation, it is clear that his examination of Tausret's temple site was nowhere near sufficient to serve as the basis to form any conclusions regarding the level of completion achieved in the building of the structure, or its relevance for our understanding of the reign of Tausret herself.

So it should not be surprising that our own excavation has produced, for the first time, not only an accurate plan of the monument (and, of course, a great many artifacts from Tausret's time) but also an understanding of much

The Temple Foundation Inscription

Inscriptions found by the University of Arizona Egyptian Expedition on the temple's foundation blocks (Figure 5.4)—in what was evidently a key area for the foundation ceremonies—are of particular importance for understanding Tausert's temple. The hieratic text of the first inscription found is in two rows, of which the first is more legible than the second, but the inscription (Figure 5.5) clearly contains a regnal date formula from Tausret's eighth year (including her regency with Siptah), which doubtless marks the date of the monument's founding or its expansion as a new stone temple from an original brick-built structure. The text also gives the actual name of the temple which was unknown before the inscription's discovery. The text reads: First line: *rnp.t-sp 8, I šmw 24* —"Regnal year eight, first month of summer, day 24." Second line: [...] *ʿn mi Sth nḫt*—apparently meaning, "[The temple?] beautiful like Seth the strong one [or, like Sethnakht]...." (see note 12).

This text is very important for the history of the temple, not only because it dates artifacts found in the foundation level of the temple very precisely, but also because of what it suggests about the queen's reign as pharaoh. While most recent works give the length of Tausret's reign as being only eight years (including her six-year regency with Siptah), this is based on the latest known documents from her reign which are dated to the queen's eighth year (see note 13). However, a temple for King Siptah had been constructed during the queen's regency, and it is unlikely that Tausret would have waited two years into her independent reign to begin work on her own temple. Tausret could thus have begun a small brick-built temple early in her independent reign and then gone on to have foundations laid for a more extensive, stone-built structure later. In any event, the date of the foundation inscription (closely paralleled in another more recently discovered text) in the queen's eighth year—in conjunction with the evidence that at least one and more probably two years of building were accomplished on this temple—indicates a longer reign for Tausret (of at least nine, and possibly ten or more, years) than has been previously realized.

further building development than has been suspected and new insights into Tausret's reign.

This evidence may be best seen in considering the developmental stages that we have discovered in the temple's construction. While some elements of the temple may have been constructed contemporaneously with others in the course of the building program, the various phases[16] are generally sequential and follow the history of the temple itself.

An Initial Mud Brick Structure?

It has sometimes been presumed that Tausret first built a small mud brick structure[17] for herself—perhaps even as early as when she acted as regent during the reign of Siptah, or at least at the beginning of her sole rule. Interestingly, although we have found large amounts of New Kingdom mud brick at the rear of the temple area, we know now that—apart from the brick-built foundation trench walls—the brick walls built on surface areas of the site are almost all the remains of structures built long after Tausret's reign (although with bricks taken from brick-built storage buildings that were apparently constructed on the north[18] side of the temple in Tausret's time, as we will see).[19]

In any event, if an early brick temple did exist, most if not all evidence of it would doubtless have been removed when Tausret later decided that a larger and grander stone structure should be constructed. But there are some indications that such an early brick temple did exist. A graffito found in the temple of Thutmose III at nearby Deir el-Bahari and dated to the second month of summer in Tausret's seventh year specifically mentions a visit of the god Amun's statue to the queen's temple during the "Beautiful Feast of the Valley" in that year.[20] As we now know that the foundations for Tausret's stone temple were not even begun till a full year later—in her eighth year—we can only presume that the visit mentioned in the graffito was to an earlier brick temple that was already in place.

Archaeologically, then, although we have no direct proof that Tausret had an earlier brick temple built in her own honor, there are reasons to believe that this was the case. Yet another indication that such an early brick temple had been built might be seen in another way.

Making Space for a Larger Temple

Before the building of a stone temple was begun by Tausret, a section of the rock escarpment that rises behind the temple site was cut away. As Petrie noted in his summary report, the temple of Tausret was positioned in such a manner that a section of the escarpment running along the west of the temple site had to be cut back to accommodate the northwest corner of the temple structure.[21] In January of 2011 we excavated this area to confirm the situation and the clearly cut rock was revealed. It is extremely unlikely that this time-consuming and work-intensive cut was made for an initial mud brick temple—which is by definition an economical structure and which could simply have been built further out from the escarpment. It is much more likely that this cut was made to accommodate the enlargement of an original mud brick temple, the area of which was now sanctified, into an expanded stone structure. On the other hand, the broad shelf on which Tausret's temple stood was amply large enough for the stone-built temple without the need for such cutting of the escarpment.

Foundations for a Stone Temple

Once Tausret had decided on the exact location of her stone-built temple, deep and well-cut foundation trenches were dug over the whole site. These trenches varied in depth—being deeper on the sides of the temple and around the courtyard area, where the highest walls would be built—but were in most cases at least 1.5 meters in depth. There is no question that these trenches were large enough to hold substantial foundations capable of supporting large stone walls, and that the cutting of the network of foundation trenches was completed.

It was at this point that a number of foundation deposit pits were cut and stocked with plaques, models, amulets, and various other offerings at fairly symmetrically located points around the site. Small amulets and beads were

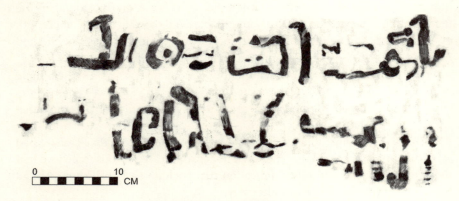

FIGURE 5.5 Drawing of the foundation inscription containing an important date formula for Tausret. Drawing by Lyla Pinch Brock, UAEE.

sprinkled not only around the pits (as Petrie stated) but also throughout most of the temple's foundation trenches, in some areas along with other artifacts in small groups or clusters that may have represented "mini-offerings."

Also, at some point before or after the placing of foundation deposits, the small, trench-spanning mud brick walls (with bricks possibly being reused from the earlier brick temple) were built every 1.5–2 meters throughout the foundation trenches, probably to stabilize the foundation sand that would be poured into the trenches, as already suggested. The only areas where we did not find these walls were usually disturbed parts of the site where Petrie's men evidently removed them in the course of digging for foundation pits. And in those areas, scattered mud bricks—clearly the remains of the walls—were usually found in the debris that we removed.

Once these walls were in place, Tausret's workmen placed a deep (c. 1 m) bed of clean sand in all the trenches to receive foundation stones. Large foundation blocks would then have been placed in all of the trenches throughout the temple. Because we have found whole, partial, and fragmentary foundation blocks throughout the trenches, as we have excavated them, we are confident that all the trenches did indeed receive foundation blocks, although most seem to have been removed at a later time. The complete foundation blocks we have uncovered are of substantial size (e.g., 1.8 × 1.2 × .7 m) and weigh several tons. They are similar to foundation blocks found in other stone temples of the Theban area and commensurate with the size necessary for the heavy load bearing of large stone walls. The important inscriptions found on two of these foundation blocks, which are dated to Tausret's eighth regnal year, clearly position the foundation phase of the temple's building as having occurred in the independent reign of Tausret as Pharaoh.[22] This delay beyond the beginning of her independent rule would certainly mesh with an understanding of the queen's rebuilding and expanding an earlier brick temple.

Building the Stone Temple

Petrie compared the plan of Tausret's temple with that of Merenptah, its closest neighbor to the south. But this comparison was based to at least some extent on his faulty mapping of the Tausret temple's foundation trenches. Our excavations have revealed that Tausret actually copied far more closely the innermost area of the core of the temple of Ramesses II, the Ramesseum,[23] (and its alignment)[24]—just as she emulated that king's royal cartouches in her own. But Petrie's comparison is instructive in another way, that of the relative size of the queen's monument. Regarding the size of the temple's entrance pylon Petrie wrote: "This pylon would have been 110 × 20 or 24 cubits, against 120 × 20 in Merenptah's [temple], or 132 × 20 in the Ramesseum."[25] The overall area of Tausret's temple also closely approximated that of Merenptah's monument, as Petrie noted too.[26] It is as though the queen wished her own temple to be at least as large as that of the son and successor of Ramesses even if she could not match the size of the great king's edifice.

Although it has long been presumed that no more than the foundation trenches were constructed on Tausret's temple site, with a very few foundation stones being placed in them, there is actually considerable evidence for the completion or near-completion of the temple. Petrie does not mention the presence of superstructure building stones on the site—only "a few foundation blocks"; but we found a complete building stone (some .70 × .52 × .26 m)[27] sitting on top of a foundation block in one undisturbed area and many fragments of building blocks throughout the site. A number of these chunks of broken stone have two or more corner angles at distances showing they could not be parts of the much larger foundation blocks and that the blocks from which they came were, in fact, commensurate with the size of building blocks. Considering that most of the large foundation stones were apparently later pried from the trenches and removed, the smaller size, accessibility, and relatively easy extraction of building blocks explain why virtually none of these blocks would have remained on the site.

A key indicator of the advanced completion of the building of a stone structure may be seen in what modern Egyptians call *dekka*—mud-gypsum flooring—which we found in patches of various sizes on most of the floor surfaces we have uncovered, indicating that walls had already been built around these areas, as the *dekka* floor surfaces would have been destroyed in the building process if they had been put in before the walls were built.

In addition to the presence of mud-gypsum flooring on surface areas, plaster found on and around many of the stone chunks we uncovered also indicates that walls and other features were built and plastered before being later demol-ished for their stone. The presence of plastered walls would indicate roofing was in place on the temple, as no one would plaster a wall before the roof was built.[28] Most of the plaster is undecorated, however, suggesting that while the temple had been largely structurally completed, decoration had been begun in perhaps only a few areas before the work was halted. This fact represents a tantalizing clue to the point in her reign at which Tausret died naturally or was overthrown in a power struggle which led to the rule of Sethnakht and dynastic change.

Construction of Ancillary Temple Structures

Our analysis of satellite images of the site early in our investigation[29] suggested the possible presence of outlying ancillary structures around the core of the Tausret temple. For example, directly along the side of the temple at the north-west, the outline of features resembling brick-built storage magazines seems to be apparent. Limited physical investigation carried out in our 2009–2010 and 2010–2011 excavation seasons confirmed the corners and edges of mud brick structures—most likely magazines—in this area, and it is hoped that a recently completed remote sensing survey, utilizing ground penetrating radar, will identify other features that may be present in the temple site. These other

Reconstructing the Completed Temple of Tausret

Although the evidence that has been recovered clearly demonstrates that Tausret's temple must have been completed or nearly so, we may never know exactly what features were completed and what were not. Given the plan of the temple that it has been possible to establish, and the archaeo-logical evidence found in various parts of the site, the computer-generated model shown here indicates how the completed temple may well have looked (Figure 5.6). While details of the wall or second pylon at the rear of the temple's open court cannot be established, and even the presence of columns around the court cannot be known for sure, this reconstruction faithfully follows the temple's plan and is our best approximation of how the completed temple might have looked. At the far side (northwest) of the temple the brick-built storage magazines can be seen in which sup-plies and offerings were kept. Directly opposite the magazines at the tem-ple's southwest corner a rectangular structure may have been a cistern cut down to the water table to provide water for the temple and the purifi-cation of its priests. Yet other features and details may perhaps be found in future excavations, but the general appearance of the core of Tausret's temple is now known.

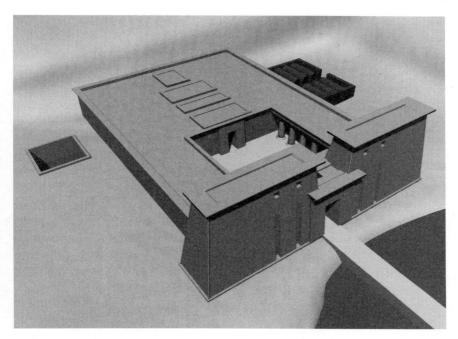

FIGURE 5.6 Hypothetical reconstruction of the completed temple of Tausret based on the findings of current excavations. Computer-generated model by Aaryn S. Brewer, UAEE.

possible sub-surface features suggested by straight lines and angles on the satellite images (and hopefully to be clarified by our remote sensing data) might include a water source (i.e., for the priests' ritual ablutions and other needs for water) and another clearly rectangular feature a little to the south of the temple proper but apparently connected to the main temple structure by a straight path. Today's archaeologists do not attempt to excavate every inch (or square meter) of a site but prefer to leave some selected areas for future researchers who will doubtless have better and more advanced methods of analysis at their disposal. As a result, we will probably leave these ancillary structures for future workers to examine, but their presence as parts of the temple complex seems clear.

Demolition of the Temple

At some point after work ceased on the decoration of Tausret's temple, the structure was evidently quarried for its building stone in the endless cycling (or recycling!) of materials that claimed, in part or in whole, so many monumental structures in ancient Egypt. Damage to the edges of many of the bedrock carved foundation trenches would suggest that over much of the site a number of large foundation stones were pried and dragged out of the trenches. This damage is especially noticeable on both sides of the temple courtyard where the trenches were more deeply cut to receive the more substantial foundations for the front of the temple. We have found a number of abandoned foundation stones in precisely this area that were broken or stuck at incongruous angles within the trenches after unsuccessful efforts to remove them.

Beyond the evident removal of the foundation blocks, both an initial surface survey carried out in our first season and our ongoing excavations have revealed the presence of thousands of dressed stone fragments over the whole site. As mentioned, many of these stone fragments have two or more corner angles at short distances or they bear plaster on one surface, indicating that they are parts of building blocks from the constructed temple. The fragments are invariably broken (not cut) from larger dressed stones, also indicating that stone features were forcefully demolished on the temple site on a widespread basis. Widespread damage to the *dekka*-coated floors of the temple's rooms is commensurate with this event. Because decoration of the temple's walls had apparently only just begun, the great majority of reused blocks from this site would unfortunately not be recognized in other buildings. Thus, whether the stone foundation and building blocks of Tausret's temple were robbed by her immediate successor Sethnakht, by his son Ramesses III, or by some later individual monarch—or several monarchs over time—is not clear. The usurpation of Tausret's tomb in the Valley of the Kings by Ramesses III for the burial of his father, Sethnakht, makes the earlier king's appropriation of the stone from the queen's monument seem perhaps unlikely, and no temple is known for Sethnakht. It is perhaps more probable that the temple of Tausret was demolished by Ramesses III so the stones could be used in the building of his own great temple at Medinet Habu, though later kings may have also contributed to the destruction of the queen's monument. The notably different degrees of exposure weathering exhibited by the inner and outer temple areas might possibly suggest that two stages of demolition were involved, but this is difficult to ascertain.

Later Intrusive Structures

Interestingly, the site of Tausret's temple seems to have been viewed as a sacred area long after the monument's destruction. Petrie recorded the presence of some "late" tombs cut into the escarpment at the rear (west) of the temple, and our excavations have brought to light a great deal of evidence of one or more of these tombs. In 2010–2011 we uncovered the entrance to one of the tombs, and we have found not only the disarticulated remains of eight or more mummified individuals[30] but also a good deal of material from their associated burials in the area directly outside the tomb where the contents of the burial were apparently divided by robbers at some time in the past. The pottery and funerary fragments from this assemblage are of the Late Period,[31] hundreds of years after the building of the temple itself. In the same area in which we discovered these remains, close to the entrances of the tombs themselves, a number of surfaces that we have examined at the rear of the temple have mud brick structures well above the level of the New Kingdom floor surfaces, and these structures seem to represent the remains of Late Period funerary chapels, courts, and other buildings associated with the burials. More work needs to be done to understand this evidence, but it is clear that the later intrusive burials and their associated structures show that the temple site—even though long destroyed—was still regarded as a sacred area, close to the gods, for the purposes of burial.

Rediscovery of a "Temple of Millions of Years"

The excavation conducted by the UAEE at the Tausret temple site has firmly established that the site was not properly investigated by Petrie in 1896 and that any conclusion regarding the unfinished nature of the temple based on Petrie's work is unfounded. The Expedition's work has also led to an understanding of the developmental stages in the history of the temple, as described here. It is of considerable archaeological and historical importance that the evidence uncovered points to Tausret's temple having been far more developed than has previously been believed, and that the monument was doubtless completed, or nearly completed, then demolished for its stone by Sethnakht, Ramesses III, or another king or kings after Tausret disappeared from view.

We may never know whether her temple was immediately torn down or if it lay open and deserted before being finally mined for its stone. But whatever the exact nature of the demise of this queen may have been—and the subsequent destruction of her temple—the history of the structure as revealed by our excavations fits well with what is known of the turbulent times in which Tausret lived and ruled. Our new understandings of many of the details of this temple—such as its previously unknown name, as well as confirmation that the monument was patterned on the inner temple of Ramesses II and that the queen's reign was longer than had been realized—are all great advances beyond our previous knowledge of Tausret and her "temple of millions of years."

Afterword

RICHARD H. WILKINSON AND
CATHARINE H. ROEHRIG

Although Tausret's reign seems to have ended abruptly and to have been followed by the usurpation of her tomb and the destruction of her temple, the queen's name lived on—if tenuously—in later texts. But resurrection of the memory of Tausret would not occur for another three thousand years.

In modern times the queen's name resurfaced sometimes in unlikely ways. The first glimpse of Tausret came with the advent of Egyptology in the opening third of the nineteenth century. Many of the tombs in the Valley of the Kings were at least partially accessible when the first European travelers visited Egypt. In 1829, the great French Egyptologist, Jean-François Champollion, visited the Valley and was able to identify the owner of one tomb as a queen named Tahoser (his reading of Tausret's name) who had ruled Egypt as pharaoh.

Nearly three decades later, in 1857, another Frenchman, Théophile Gautier, wrote a novel entitled *Le Roman de la Momie,* or *The Romance of the Mummy.*[1] At the beginning of the story, a young Englishman and his Egyptologist traveling companion discover an undisturbed tomb in the Valley of the Kings. When the sarcophagus is opened, they are astonished to find a woman's coffin and speculate on how this female came to be buried in a king's tomb. Inside the coffin is the mummy of a beautiful young woman who is so well preserved that she appears merely to be asleep. A papyrus in the coffin relates the story of the young woman, Tahoser, who rises from obscurity to become the ruler of Egypt during troubled times. The story, though inspired by Tausret, bears little relation to her life and times. However, the popularity of the novel, which was

translated into several languages and reprinted in a number of different illustrated editions well into the twentieth century, demonstrates the fascination
generated by studies of ancient Egypt and by the romantic fantasies suggested
by its powerful queens.

Since that time, Petrie's discovery of the queen's temple site and the
archaeological and historical research that have followed in the subsequent
century have certainly caused her name, as the ancient Egyptians themselves
would have said, "to live again." Even though her successors made every effort
to expunge the memory of this queen—typified by the way in which her image
was deleted from the symbolically revivifying "Opening of the Mouth" scene in
her own tomb (see Figure A.1 in insert)—we now have a greater understanding
of the life and reign of Tausret than would have been dreamed possible a few
decades ago. As this book has shown, in the last few years we have come to see
many aspects of the nature of Tausret's relationship with other rulers of her
age and the manner in which she rose steadily in power to eventually become
pharaoh herself. We now not only understand much of the ideology that developed to accompany that progression to power, but also we have a better sense
of the longer reign which she evidently enjoyed and have recovered many more
details of both the queen and her times. We have new evidence of Tausret's
reign found in places quite distant from Egypt, and a better sense of her importance in her own land. Yet many questions remain, of course, and some seem
tantalizingly close to being answered—but not just yet.

Research on Tausret continues apace, and new approaches should produce
better understanding in areas as diverse as the psychological motivation of this
powerful woman and the nature of her actual status and levels of respect within
her own governmental apparatus and among the people at large. The combination of Tausret's mention in Homer and chance archaeological finds has
enabled us to catch glimpses of Tausret's relations with foreign lands, but how
extensive were these? Was this queen particularly interested in foreign contacts, or no more so than other rulers of her age? These questions, and others
like them, will require new knowledge to answer, but all hinge on the kind of
woman she was and the level of her accomplishments.

Perhaps foremost among the questions that still remain regarding Tausret
we must ask what became of this queen who ruled as pharaoh. We do not
have her mummified remains and neither extant historical evidence nor the
results of the excavation of Tausret's tomb or temple can presently tell us
whether she died peacefully or was overthrown by her successor Sethnakht.
Certainly, dynastic change occurred when her rule came to an end, and it may
be expecting too great a coincidence to believe that this dynastic change happened without a power struggle occurring at the same time. On the other hand,
it remains possible that Tausret died a natural death and the lack of any clear
heir led to a simple seizure of power by Sethnakht. The paucity of texts from
this period may mean that the situation will always remain an elusive question

of history—the end of the 19th Dynasty is, after all, one of the murkier periods of the New Kingdom era, and it is likely that it will remain so. Nevertheless, the often surprising results of the excavations discussed in this book and the added understandings gained from the in-depth research behind its chapters show that new information may still come to light in one way or another and that new light may yet be shed on this difficult period in unexpected ways.

As it is, we do now understand much more about the reign of this important woman than was possible even a relatively few years ago, and it is no exaggeration to say that she may now more firmly claim the position of one of ancient Egypt's most important women—one of the very few who, in the many thousands of years of ancient Egyptian history, acted, built, inscribed, and ruled as female pharaohs.

Notes

INTRODUCTION

1. This fact is made clear in Aidan Dodson, *Poisoned Legacy: The Fall of the Nineteenth Egyptian Dynasty* (Cairo: American University in Cairo Press, 2010).

2. Gardiner, Alan H. "Only One King Siptah and Twosre Not His Wife," *Journal of Egyptian Archaeology* 44 (1958): 12–22

3. See, for example, Heather Lee McCarthy's recent study, "Rules of Decorum and Expressions of Gender Fluidity in Tawosret's Tomb," in *Sex and Gender in Ancient Egypt: "Don Your Wig for a Joyful Hour,"* ed. C. Graves-Brown (Swansea: Classical Press of Wales, 2008), 83–113.

CHAPTER 1

1. For an introduction to the role of women in ancient Egypt, consult Betsy M. Bryan, *Mistress of the House, Mistress of Heaven: Women in Ancient Egypt* (New York: Hudson Hill Press, 1997). See also Gay Robins, *Women in Ancient Egypt* (London: British Museum Press, 1993); and Joyce A. Tyldesley, *Daughters of Isis: Women of Ancient Egypt* (New York: Viking/Penguin, 1994).

2. Briefly discussed in Grajetzki, *Ancient Egyptian Queens*, 1.

3. Lichtheim, *Ancient Egyptian Literature I*, 61–80.

4. There is still considerable debate over the exact calendar dates of the reigns of Egypt's earliest pharaohs. It is not until 672 BCE, with the 26th Dynasty reign of Psamtek I, that we can give dates with absolute precision. To ensure consistency, the dates given in this chapter are all taken from the chronology given in Ian Shaw, ed., *Oxford History of Ancient Egypt* (Oxford: Oxford University Press, 2000), 479–483.

5. *Maat* is a concept with no literal English translation. It is often defined as a combination of abstracts including justice, truth, order, and the status quo. Its

opposite, *isfet*, or chaos, is far easier for us to understand. *Maat* was personified in the form of the goddess Maat, daughter of the sun god, who wore the feather of truth on her head.

6. For an extensive discussion of pharaoh's role throughout the dynastic age, consult the papers by various authorities in David O'Connor and David P. Silverman, eds., *Ancient Egyptian Kingship* (Leiden: Brill, 1995).

7. To take a few specific New Kingdom examples: the 18th- Dynasty pharaoh Ay is likely to have been well into his sixties at his accession; his predecessor, Tutankhamen, is unlikely to have been more than eight years old at his. The 19th- Dynasty mummy of Siptah reveals that he had a shortened left leg, yet he appears without this handicap in his official art; the founder of the 19th Dynasty, Ramesses I, was an elderly commoner when he inherited the throne.

8. Manetho, preserved in Africanus and Eusebius, explains that during the 2nd Dynasty it was decided that women "might hold the kingly office." As 1st Dynasty Egypt had already experienced female rule, it seems that this was confirmation of an already established practice. See W. G. Waddell, *Manetho* (Cambridge, MA: Loeb Classical Library, 1940), 37 and 39.

9. Discussed in more detail in Lana Troy, *Patterns of Queenship in Ancient Egyptian Myth and History* (Uppsala: Acta Universitatis Upsaliensis, 1986). For an examination of the lives of individual queen-consorts, see Joyce A. Tyldesley, *Chronicle of the Queens of Egypt: From Early Dynastic Times to the Death of Cleopatra* (London: Thames and Hudson, 2006).

10. Gay Robins, "A Critical Examination of the Theory that the Right to the Throne of Egypt Passed through the Female Line in the 18th Dynasty," *Göttinger Miszellen* 62 (1983): 67–77.

11. Joyce A. Tyldesley, *Myths and Legends of Ancient Egypt* (London: Viking/Penguin, 2010).

12. The king's *serekh* was usually topped by a falcon—symbol of the god Horus. In the Old Kingdom the *serekh* would be replaced by the cartouche, an oval loop drawn around the royal nomen and prenomen.

13. W. M. Flinders Petrie, *Royal Tombs of the First Dynasty*, Vol. I (London: Egypt Exploration Society, 1900).

14. She was, however, excluded from the necropolis seal of Qaa, which lists the 1st Dynasty kings. For full references to the evidence for the "reign" of Meritneith, see Toby Wilkinson, *Early Dynastic Egypt* (London: Routledge, 1999), 74–75.

15. The shared roof indicates that their bodies were buried at the same time; this does not necessarily mean that they all died at the same time. So there remains a possibility that some, or all, of these graves housed reburials.

16. See, for example, Émile Amélineau, *Les Nouvelles Fouilles D'Abydos 1895–1898* (Paris: Ernest Leroux, 1899), plates XXXIV–XXXVII.

17. Florence D. Friedman, "The Menkaure Dyad(s)," in *Egypt and Beyond: Essays Presented to Leonard H. Lesko*, ed. Stephen E. Thompson and Peter Der Manuelian (Providence, RI: Department of Egyptology, Brown University, 2008), 109–144.

18. Turin Museum: Illustrated in Tyldesley, *Chronicle of the Queens of Egypt*, 38.

19. Tomb G8978. See Barbara S. Lesko, "Queen Kharmerernebty II and Her Sculpture," in *Ancient Egyptian and Mediterranean Studies in Memory of William A Ward*, ed. Leonard H. Lesko (Providence, RI: Brown University, 1998), 149–162.

20. See, for example, George A. Reisner and William Stevenson Smith, *A History of the Giza Necropolis II: The Tomb of Hetepheres the Mother of Cheops* (Cambridge, MA: Harvard University Press, 1955); Mark Lehner, *The Pyramid Tomb of Hetepheres and the Satellite Pyramid of Khufu* (Mainz: Philipp von Zabern, 1985).

21. Tomb LG100.

22. Miroslav Verner, *The Pyramids: Their Archaeology and History*, trans. Steven Rendall (London: Atlantic Books, 2002), 259–264.

23. For a full translation, see Miriam Lichtheim, *Ancient Egyptian Literature I: The Old and Middle Kingdoms* (Berkeley: University of California Press, 1974), 215–222.

24. Miroslav Verner, *Abusir*, Vol. III. *The Pyramid Complex of Khentkaus* (Praha: Czech Institute of Egyptology, 1995).

25. Herodotus, *The Histories*, Vol. II, trans. A. de Sélincourt, rev. with introduction and notes by J. Marincola (London: Viking/Penguin, 1996), 100.

26. Robyn A. Gillam, "Priestesses of Hathor: Their Function, Decline and Disappearance," *Journal of the American Research Centre in Egypt* 32 (1995): 211–237.

27. For an examination of queens' titles, see Wolfram Grajetzki, *Ancient Egyptian Queens: A Hieroglyphic Dictionary* (London: Golden House Publications, 2005).

28. Today Ptahnofru's own pyramid is waterlogged and almost totally destroyed. It has been investigated by Labib Habachi (1936) and Naguib Farag (1950s) and has yielded grave goods including an offering table, silver vessels, pots, and a granite sarcophagus.

29. Louvre Museum E27135.

30. Metropolitan Museum 65.59.1.

31. Our increased knowledge about the deeds of the New Kingdom queens is, of course, helped by the better state of preservation of the Theban monuments.

32. Cairo Museum CG 34009.

33. The evidence concerning the burials of Ahhotep I and II is confusing. See Lana Troy, "Ahhotep—A Source Evaluation," *Göttinger Miszellen* 35 (1979): 81–91.

34. Hatshepsut has been the subject of many books and articles. Information presented here is drawn from Catharine H. Roehrig, ed., *Hatshepsut: From Queen to Pharaoh. Exhibition Catalogue* (New York: Metropolitan Museum of Art, 2005); and Joyce A. Tyldesley, *Hatchepsut: The Female Pharaoh* (London: Viking/Penguin, 1996).

35. See Édouard Naville, *The Temple of Deir el-Bahari*, 7 volumes (London: Egypt Exploration Fund, 1895–1908).

36. Hatshepsut counted her regnal years from the accession of Thutmose III. So, although she died in Year 22, she ruled for fifteen years. Her date of death is recorded on a stela at Armant (*Urk IV*: 1244): Suzanne Ratié, *La Reine Hatchepsout: Sources et Problèmes* (Leiden: E.J. Brill, 1979), 295–296.

37. See C. Blankenberg-Van Delden, *The Large Commemorative Scarabs of Amenhotep III* (Leiden: Brill, 1969); also C. Blankenberg-Van Delden, "More Large Commemorative Scarabs of Amenophis III," *Journal of Egyptian Archaeology* 62 (1976): 74–80.

38. William L. Moran, *The Amarna Letters* (Baltimore, MD: Johns Hopkins University Press, 1992).

39. An image of Tiy in the form of a winged sphinx wearing the crown of Tefnut decorates a carnelian plaque housed in the Metropolitan Museum of Art, New York (26.7.1342).

40. There remains the possibility that Sitamen married her brother, the heir to the throne, Thutmose.

41. Details concerning Nefertiti's life and role are taken from Joyce A. Tyldesley, *Nefertiti: Egypt's Sun Queen*, rev. ed. (London: Viking/Penguin, 2005).

42. Discussed in Dorothea Arnold, "Aspects of the Royal Female Image during the Amarna Period," in *The Royal Women of Amarna: Images of Beauty from Ancient Egypt*, ed. Dorothea Arnold (New York: Metropolitan Museum of Art, 1996), 85–119.

43. See Lyn Green, "Queen as Goddess: The Religious Role of Royal Women in the Late-Eighteenth Dynasty," *Amarna Letters* 1 (1992): 28–41.

44. For the argument that Nefertiti may have ruled as pharaoh, see, for example, Aidan Dodson, *Amarna Sunset: Nefertiti, Tutankhamun, Ay, Horemheb and the Egyptian Counterrevolution* (Cairo: American University in Cairo Press, 2009). For the argument that she died at Amarna, see Tyldesley, *Nefertiti*, 139–166.

45. Translation based on Guterbock, as quoted in Alan R. Schulman, "Ankhesenamun, Nofretity and the Amka Affair," *Journal of the American Research Centre in Egypt* 15 (1978): 43–48.

46. For full details of the plot against Ramesses III, see Susan Redford, *The Harem Conspiracy: The Murder of Ramesses III* (Dekalb: Northern Illinois University Press, 2002).

47. Adrian De Buck, "The Judicial Papyrus of Turin," *Journal of Egyptian Archaeology* 23:2 (1937): 152–164.

48. *Papyrus Rollin*. Translation based on that given in Hans Goedicke, "Was Magic Used in the Harem Conspiracy against Ramesses III?" *Journal of Egyptian Archaeology* 49 (1963): 71–92.

49. The earliest references to this myth include hymns, non-narrative fragments of funerary texts, and illustrations. The cryptic *Great Hymn to Osiris*, carved on the 18th- Dynasty stela of Amenmose (Louvre Museum C286), is our most complete, purely Egyptian version: see Miriam Lichtheim, *Ancient Egyptian Literature II: The New Kingdom* (Berkeley: University of California Press, 1976), 81–86. Diodorus Siculus preserves a short version of the myth in his *Histories* I: 21 (Diodorus Siculus, *Library of History I*, trans. C. H. Oldfather [Cambridge, MA: Loeb Classical Library, 1933]). Our most detailed account comes from Plutarch's *De Iside et Osiride* (Plutarch, *Isis and Osiris*, *Moralia V*, trans. F. C. Babbitt [Cambridge, MA: Loeb Classical Library, 1936]). This, written in c. AD 120, adds Roman influences to the tale.

50. Information on the life and times of Cleopatra VII is taken from Joyce A. Tyldesley, *Cleopatra: Egypt's Last Queen* (London: Profile Books, 2008).

CHAPTER 2

1. E.g., the letter from the King of Ugarit to the King of Alashia (RS 20.238): see M. Astour, "The Last Days of Ugarit," *American Journal of Archaeology* 69 (1965): 255.

2. On these people, see D. B. Redford, *Egypt, Canaan and Israel in Ancient Times* (Princeton, NJ: Princeton University Press, 1992), 243ff.

3. The numbers are confusing, not least because of lacunae in our sources. How much is exaggeration is incalculable.

4. M. Eaton-Krauss, "Sety-Merenptah als Kronprinz Merenptahs," *Göttinger Miszellen* 50 (1981): 15–21. Particularly interesting is her recording of the unique title for

the prince, *ḥrp t3wj n jtj.f* as well as *r-pʿt m st Gb* (p.19), both titles indicating his selection as the aging Merenptah's deputy.

5. Frank J. Yurko, "Amenmesse: Six Statues at Karnak," *Metropolitan Museum Journal* 14 (1979): 15–31.

6. In the opinion of Jac. J. Janssen (*Village Varia, Ten Studies in the History and Administration of Deir el Medina* [Leiden: Nederlands Instituut voor het nabije Oosten, 1997], 106), big changes in the names of workers in the royal tombs indicate to him that a purge of workers took place when Sety II returned to power.

7. E.g., M. Bierbrier, *The Tomb-builders of the Pharaohs* (London: British Museum Publications, 1982), 107.

8. For example, J. E. Harris and E. F. Wente, *An X-Ray Atlas of the Royal Mummies* (Chicago: University of Chicago Press, 1980), 146, remark that a queen named Takhat is named on a statue (CG 1198) of Merenptah as *King's Daughter, King's Great Wife, who has joined with her Horus, Takhat.* Her titles have not been touched. See also A. Dodson, "The Takhats and Some Other Royal Ladies of the Ramesside Period," *Journal of Egyptian Archaeology* 73 (1987): 224–229.

9. E. C. Brock, "The Sarcophagus Lid of Queen Takhat," in *Egyptology at the Dawn of the Twenty-first Century: Archaeology*, ed. Z. Hawass and L. Pinch Brock, Vol. I (Cairo: American University in Cairo Press, 2000), 99. E. C. Brock has revealed that the sarcophagus of this queen had been usurped from a royal woman named Anuket-em-heb, a probable daughter of Ramesses II. The titles of the original owner had been changed for Takhat, who is entitled: *King's Great Wife.* R. C. Lepsius (*Denkmäler aus Ägypten und Äthiopien*, Vol. 3 [Leipzig: Édouard Naville, 1900], 202 f, g) reproduces the wall reliefs from Amenmesse's tomb showing both queens Takhat and Baketwerel. E. Thomas (*The Royal Necropoleis of Thebes*, private printing, [Princeton, 1966], 111) writes that the only Baketwerel known to her was apparently the wife of Ramesses XI. Yurko'sassumption ("Amenmesse," 23) that the queen depicted on one of the six Karnak statues is Baketwerel is unfounded: there are no traces of any name for the queen on that statue. Thomas points out that the decoration of the rooms where the queens are depicted is far different from the original quality of decoration by Amenmesse and this, too, should be taken into account. The statements of the current excavators report that the tomb decoration is secondary, suggesting that these women were later queens (see the website of the Amenmesse Project for details, http://www.kv-10.com). Only this later queen Takhat appears to have been interred in KV-10, in the vaulted chamber (G), which served as her burial chamber. The fragment of a sarcophagus lid found in KV 10 with Takhat's name, therefore, probably did not belong to Amenmesse's mother. See also A. Dodson's article, "The Takhats."

10. Yurko, "Amenmesse," 15–31.

11. Yurko, "Amenmesse," 28 and note 36. Yurko's explanation of Takhat's titles here also confirms my suspicions that Takhat had never been the wife of Sety II; it is thus likely that Tausret had been Sety's only known wife. (The claim of N. Grimal, *A History of Ancient Egypt*, trans. I. Shaw [Oxford: Blackwell Books, 1988], 269; Dodson, "The Takhats," 227, and others that Sety II had a wife named Tiaa is also unfounded.)

12. Of course, we do not know how old Tausret was at any stage, yet the age of the mummy registered as Sety II was young and the king's wife could be approximately his age. The statue of Sety II (Lepsius, *Denkmäler*, 299; Gae Callender, "The Cripple,

the Queen and the Man from the North," *KMT: A Modern Journal of Ancient Egypt* 17:1 [2006]: 52 for a full frontal photograph) does portray a youthful king, which may also be considered. Additionally, the suspicion that the queen had given birth to a child inclines also us to think of Tausret as "youthful." We cannot depend upon artwork featuring the queen to be reliable, but this is also youthful.

13. G. Elliot Smith, *Catalogue Général des Antiquités Égyptiennes du Musée du Caire Nos. 61051–61100: The Royal Mummies* (Cairo: Service des Antiquites de L'Égypte, 1912), 73.

14. Harris and Wente, *An X-Ray Atlas of the Royal Mummies*, Table 6.4 (between pp. 205 and 234), X-ray no. 50. Elsewhere in this book (p. 263), however, E. Wente says that from his calculations, Sety II would have been "approximately sixty-five years" old at his time of death—a remark that, in regard to the mummy, is not supported by the authors' detailed forensic evidence.

15. See also C. Aldred's comments supporting this view: "The Parentage of King Siptah," *Journal of Egyptian Archaeology* 49 (1963): 43.

16. C. Aldred, "The Parentage of King Siptah," *Journal of Egyptian Archaeology* 49 (1963): 41–60; see p. 45 regarding his claim.

17. L. H. Lesko, "A Little More Evidence for the End of the Nineteenth Dynasty," *Journal of the American Research Center in Egypt* 5 (1966): 31. (Lesko inclines toward Sety—although he concludes by saying that either Sety or Amenmesse could have been the father.)

18. J. R. Harris and K. Weeks, "X-raying the Pharaohs," *Natural History* (August/ September, 1972): 61.

19. A more analytical account of the genealogy for these members of the royal family can be found in V. G. Callender, "Queen Tausret and the End of Dynasty 19," *Studien zur Altägyptischen Kultur* 32 (2004): 82–85.

While the majority of scholars assume that Sety II was the father of Siptah, it has been thought that Amenmesse might be more likely. E. Wente perceptively remarks (Harris and Wente, *An X-Ray Atlas of the Royal Mummies*, 147) that "neither Amenmesse nor Siptah was included in the Medinet Habu procession of statues of ancestral kings, although Merenptah and Sety II were; such an omission leads one to suspect that Amenmesse and Siptah were linked together in being regarded as illegitimate rulers, and that therefore they were probably father and son." (This remark is based on comments by C. Aldred, "The Parentage of King Siptah," 45, where Aldred underlines the fact that both Amenmesse and Siptah had both lived in Chemmis when they were young. Aldred also rightly points out that any son of Sety's would not have been considered an illegitimate king by later rulers.)

20. R. Drenkhahn, *Die Elephantine-Stele des Sethnacht und ihr historischer Hintergrund*, Ägyptologische Abhandlung 36 (Wiesbaden: Harrassowitz, 1980), 17. Actual translation of the hieroglyphs would usually be rendered as, "Great Female Speaker of the Pat/nobility"; customary translations of titles are often traditional renditions and not exact equivalents of the Egyptian terms.

21. The royal tombs found in the Valley of the Kings are conventionally designated by "KV" (King's Valley) numbers—from KV1 to KV63—following the system established by the nineteenth-century British Egyptologist Sir John Gardner Wilkinson.

22. See Chapter 4 in the present volume.

23. J. von Beckerath, "Queen Twosre as Guardian of Siptah," *Journal of Egyptian Archaeology* 48 (1962): 70–74.

24. R. Drenkhahn, "Ein Nachtrag zur Tausret," *Göttinger Miszellen* 43 (1981): 19ff.

25. R. Krauss, "Untersuchungen zu König Amenmesse (1. Teil)," *Studien zur Altägyptischen Kultur* 4 (1976): 188, note 88.

26. For the report on this tomb, see T. M. Davis, G. Maspero, E. Ayrton, et al., *The Tomb of Siptah; The Monkey Tomb and the Gold Tomb* (London: A. Constable, 1908), 2ff., 31ff. C. Aldred, "The Parentage from King Siptah," 177, suggested that the burial had been for a child and that Tausret's jewelry had been one of the usual "heirloom" gifts deposited with the body during the funeral.

27. For a report on a recent excavation of Tomb 56, see the text of a lecture delivered in London by Nicholas Reeves, "Re-excavating 'The Gold Tomb,'" *Valley of the Kings: The Amarna Royal Tombs Project 1998–2001, 29 September 2001* [online] available at http://www.nicholasreeves.com/item. In the opinion of Reeves, this tomb, originally, could have been intended for some Amarna person—perhaps Kiya—but his finds from this second clearance are not conclusive. He does not mention the names of Sety II and Tausret in his talk. However, he did find evidence of a coffin burial—merely fragments—which he attributed to an Amarna wooden coffin.

28. If the theory that Amenmesse was actually the father of Siptah is correct, then this, too, would have had decisive consequences. Nothing is certain about this issue.

29. J. Černý and A. H. Gardiner, *Hieratic Ostraca*, Vol. I (Oxford: Griffith Institute, 1957) 7, 3. See also Černý's later publication, "A Note on the Chancellor Bay," *Zeitschrift für Ägyptische Sprache und Altertumskunde* 93 (1966): 35–39.

30. See the argument in H. Altenmüller, "Zweiter Vorbericht über die Arbeiten des Archäologischen Instituts am Grab des Bay (KV 13) im Tal der Könige von Theben," *Studien zur Altägyptischen Kultur* 19 (1992): 29ff. Altenmüller remarks that the statement that Bay was a foreigner is caused by his name on the so-called Shellal Road, near Aswan, where his loyalist name of *Ramesses-kha-em-netjeru* is inscribed. Frequently, foreigners took on such names in addition to their own. On the one hand, W. M. Flinders Petrie, *A History of Egypt*, 4th ed. (London: Methuen, 1905), 133, considers that his name honors Ba, the ram god of Mendes, and that Bay might be from the Delta. On the other hand, K. A. Kitchen, "A Note on 'Sojourner,' a Foreign word for Foreigners in Egypt," in *Egypt and Kush. In Memoriam, Mikhail A. Korostovtsev,* ed. E. E. Kormysheda (Moscow: Nauka, 1993), 237–241, remarks that Bay uses a foreign word to describe himself as a foreigner, and Kitchen thinks the usage might even be "a sardonic joke" of Bay's in reference to his origins. In earlier remarks, G. Posener, "La complainte de l'echanson Bay," in *Fragen an die altägyptiische Literatur: Studien zum Gedenken an Eberhard Otto,* ed. J. Assmann, E. Feucht, R. Grieshammer (Wiesbaden: Ludwig Reichert, 1977), 392ff., in discussing Ostrakon CG 25766, a text thought to have been written by Bay, notes its literary character, which lends strength to Kitchen's proposal. We also observe that there is a long text written on the Deir el-Bahari Temple of Mentuhotep, only the bottom half of which survives. This text also shows literary flair—see E. Frood, *Biographical Texts from Ramessid Egypt* (Atlanta: Society of Biblical Literature, 2007), 175–177.

31. Rock inscription near Aswan, Lepsius, *Denkmäler* III, 202c; rock inscription from Gebel es-Sisileh, Lepsius, *Denkmäler* III, 202a.

32. Itamar Singer, "A Political History of Ugarit," in *Handbook of Ugaritic Studies*, ed. Wilfred Watson and Nicolas Wyatt (Leiden: Brill, 1999), 713f.

33. Singer, "A Political History of Ugarit," 715.

34. We note that, at Dendera, for example, Isis is described as "She who places her son on the throne of his father." E. Chassinat, ed., *Le temple de Dendera*, Vol. 2 (Cairo: IFAO, 1934), 36, line 10.

35. E.g., A. H. Gardiner, *Egypt of the Pharaohs* (Oxford: Clarendon Press, 1961), 277.

36. This text was not written by Bay but by the King's son of Kush, the viceroy, Sety, a most prestigious official who had been given his appointment in Year 1 of Ramesses-Siptah. The year is interesting because it suggests a new appointment—perhaps because Sety was one who approved of Siptah's coronation?

37. D. O'Connor, "New Kingdom and Third Intermediate Period, 1552–664 BC," in *Ancient Egypt, a Social History*, ed. Bruce Trigger, Barry Kemp, David O'Connor, and Allen Lloyd (Cambridge: Cambridge University Press, 1983), 229ff. It is interesting, therefore, that, in Sethnakht's reign later on, that king appointed the son of one of his army officials to be the 20th Dynasty's High Priest of Amun: the line of Roy's descendants finished with the 19th Dynasty, although they became instead Mayors of Thebes.

38. Callender, "Queen Tausret and the End of Dynasty 19," 89. This Canaanite mother would, most likely, have been a member of the local ruler's family and therefore quasi-royal; if Bay had been her brother, his own rank would certainly have seemed to him no less noble. This may have given his undoubted ambition a sharper edge.

39. Altenmüller, "Zweiter Vorbericht," 27ff.

40. H. Altenmüller, "Dritter Vorbericht über die Arbeiten des Archäologischen Instituts der Universität Hamburg am Grab des Bay (KV 13) im Tal der Könige von Theben," *Studien zur Altägyptischen Kultur* 21 (1994): 3.

41. Petrie, *A History of Egypt*, 132.

42. Drenkhahn, *die Elephantine-Stele des Sethnacht und ihr historischer Hintergrund*, Ägyptologische Abhandlung 36 (Wiesbaden: Harrosswitz, 1980).

43. Pierre Grandet, "L'execution du chancelier Bay O. IFAO 1864," *Bulletin de Institut Français d'Archéologie Orientale du Caire* 100 (2000): 341.

44. Author's translation of the text in Grandet, "L'execution du chancelier Bay," 341.

45. See H. Altenmüller, "Bermerkungen zu den neu gefundenen Daten im Grab der Königin Twosre (KV 14) im Tal der Könige von Theben," in *After Tutankhamun*, ed. C.N. Reeves (London: Routledge, 1992), 153. H. Altenmüller's statement that "the balance of power at the royal court had shifted in favor of Tausret" might perhaps be interpreted as an indication of the queen's decision to alter her tomb at that time to reflect her newly attained status; that she may have been acting as a ruler before this time is not only attested by her titles as regent, but also by the death of Bay. The testimony of KV14 is a most precious record of the career of the queen from Great Royal Wife to pharaoh.

46. J. H. Breasted, *Ancient Records of Egypt* III (Chicago: University of Chicago Press, 1906), §642–651.

47. J. von Beckerath, "Königsnamen,"*Lexikon der Ägyptologie*, Vol. III (Wiesbaden: Harrassowitz, 1980), c. 551.

48. Kenneth A. Kitchen, *Ramesside Inscriptions, Translated and Annotated, Translations*, vol. IV, *Merenptah and the Late Nineteenth Dynasty* (Oxford: Blackwell Limited, 2003), 352.9.

Curiously, her *Nebty* name has been claimed to be unknown: Gay Robins, "Queens," in *Oxford Encyclopedia of Ancient Egypt*, ed. D. B. Redford, Vol. 3 (Oxford: Oxford University Press, 2001), 108. In fact, her *Nebty* name was "Founding Egypt and conquering the Foreigners." This is preserved on the Tell ed Dab`a statue of the ruler.

49. As R. Drenkhahn, "Ein Nachtrag zur Tausret," *Göttinger Miszellen* 43 (1981), 20, had already observed.

50. E.g., Qantir foundation block (Kitchen, *Ramesside Inscriptions*, IV, 352, 353 no. 19) and Heliopolis statue (ibid., IV, 352, 356 no.20).

51. H. S .K. Bakry, "The Discovery of a Statue of Queen Twosre (1202–1194? B.C.) at Madinet Nasr, Cairo," *Revista degli Studi Oriental* 46 (1971): pl.VII. R. Drenkhahn, "Ein Nachtrag zur Tausret," 21, considers this to be a mistake, but in my opinion, it is not. The writing of Tausret's throne name in her temple deliberately deceives the viewer into thinking the name is masculine. See also note 48 in this current article. Moreover, on the Bilgai Stele, the scene at the top represents a male pharaoh (see J. von Beckerath, "Queen Twosre as Guardian of Siptah," 70, note 7). Like Sobekneferu and Hatshepsut, therefore, Tausret changed her identity from time to time.

52. J. von Beckerath, *Handbuch der ägyptischen Königsnamen*, Münchner Ägyptologische Studien 20 (Berlin: Philipp von Zabern, 1984), 243.

53. von Beckerath, *Handbuch*, 243.

54. See, for example, the discussion in von Beckerath, *Handbuch*, 24.

55. Bakry, "The Discovery of a Statue," 17–26.

56. The design of the queen's cartouches also mimicked those of Ramesses II— so much so, that Petrie thought at first he was dealing with a building erected by that king—W. M. Flinders Petrie, *Six Temples at Thebes* (London: Bernard Quaritch, 1897), 15.

57. On the statuary of Hatshepsut, see Roland Tefnin, *La statuaire d'Hatshepsout* (Brussels: Fondation égyptologique reine Elisabeth, 1979).

58. At first sight, it might be thought that Tomb 55 had been intended for Queen Tiye, as was the earlier opinion, but Marc Gabolde's closely argued analysis of Tomb 55 does give compelling reasons for rejecting Tiye as the intended owner of this tomb. (See M. Gabolde, *D'Akhenaton à Toutankhamon*, Vol. 2 [Lyon: Université Lumière-Lyon, 1998], Chapter VI, 231–276.)

59. There is an excellent guide to KV 14 at the Theban Mapping website (online) available at http://www.thebanmappingproject.com/atlas/index_kv.asp?tombID=828, which has a spoken commentary by Professor Kent Weeks. (Accessed February 2011).

60. Altenmüller, "Bemerkungen," 141–164, especially 159–161.

61. H. Altenmüller, "Das Graffito 551 aus der thebanischen Nekropole," *Studien zur Altägyptischen Kultur* 21 (1994): 4 and Abb. 2 on 5.

62. H. Altenmüller, "The Tomb of Tausret and Setnakht," in *The Treasures of the Valley of the Kings: Tombs and Temples of the Theban West Bank in Luxor*, ed. Kent R. Weeks (Vercelli: WhiteStar, 2001; Cairo: American University in Cairo Press, 2001), 228.

63. H. Altenmüller, "Das Grab der Königin Tausret im Tal der Könige von Theben," *Studien zur Altägyptischen Kultur* 10 (1983): 1–24; H. Altenmüller, "Rolle und

Bedeutung des Grabes der Königin Tausret im Königsgräbertal von Theben," *Bulletin de la Société d'Égyptologie Genève* 8 (1983): 3–11.

64. G. A. Gaballa, "Some Nineteenth Dynasty Monuments in Cairo Museum," *Bulletin de l'Institut Français d'Archéologie Orientale* 71 (1972): 134 and pl. XXVI.

65. H. Altenmüller and A. Moussa, "Die Inschrift Amenemhets II. Aus dem Ptah-Tempel von Memphis," *Studien zur Altägyptischen Kultur* 18 (1991): 1–48; M. Verner and H. Vymazalová, *Abusir*, Vol. 10., *The Pyramid Complex of Raneferef. The Papyrus Archive* (Prague: Czech Institute of Egyptology, 2006), 265 and note 146, 352–353, 382 and *passim*.

66. E. B. Pusch, "Tausret und Sethos II in der Rameses-Stadt," *Ägypten und Levante* 9 (1999): 109 note 17.

67. Pusch, "Tausret und Sethos," 101–109.

68. For further discussion on these fragments, see Pusch, "Tausret und Sethos," and Callender, "Queen Tausret," 98.

69. A. H. Gardiner, "The Stele of Bilgai," *Zeitschrift für ägyptische sprache* 50 (1912): 49–57.

70. A controversial word: it can mean a number of things. Here, it is likely to be the bureaucratic headquarters for the provisioning of the temple to the god Amun.

71. E. Frood, *Biographical Texts from Ramessid Egypt* (Atlanta: Society of Biblical Literature, 2007; Leiden: Brill, 2007), 177.

72. Petrie, *Six Temples at Thebes*, pp. 13–16, plates XXII and XXVI.

73. See W. Hayes, *Scepter of Egypt*, Vol. II, rev. ed. (New York: Metropolitan Museum of Art, 1990), 358ff.

74. M. Maree, "A Jar from Sidon with the Name of Pharaoh-Queen Tawosret," *Archaeology & History in the Lebanon* 24 (2006): 121–128.

75. F. P. M. Karg, "Geheimnisvolle Siegel," *Antike Welt* 34 (2003): 285–294. Further discussion in Callender, "The Cripple, the Queen," 61.

76. H. Altenmüller, "Das Grab der Königin Tausret," 53ff.

77. H. Altenmüller, "Das Grab der Königin Tausret," 43.

78. Drenkhahn, *Die Elephantine-Stele*, 52ff.

79. E.g., N. Grimal, *A History of Ancient Egypt* (London: Wiley-Blackwell, 1992), 270–271; R. O. Faulkner in ch. 23 in *The Cambridge Ancient History. Part 2, The Middle East and the Aegean Region, c.1380–1000 BC*, 3rd ed., ed. I.E.S. Edwards et al. (Cambridge: Cambridge University Press, 2000), 240–241; Jacobus van Dijk, "The Amarna Period and the Later New Kingdom," in *The Oxford History of Ancient Egypt*, ed. Ian Shaw (Oxford: Oxford University Press, 2000), 304.

80. The most exhaustive version is that of Pierre Grandet, *Le Papyrus Harris 1* (BM 9999) Bibliotheque d'etude, vols. 109.1–2 (Cairo: L'institut français d'archéologie orientale du Caire, 1994, 1999). There is an English edition made by J. H. Breasted, *Ancient Records of Egypt*, Vol. IV §182–412 (Chicago: University of Chicago Press, 1906)—with an extensive commentary—but it is the Historical Section §397 that contains the relevant historical information we seek.

81. Drenkhahn, *Die Elephantine-Stele*, 64–67.

82. Drenkhahn, *Die Elephantine-Stele*, 79.

83. See Hermann Kern, *Nofret, die Schone: Die Frau im Alten Ägypten*, Vol. I (Mainz: Philipp von Zabern, 1984), 181, for a photograph of Ostrakon CG 25125 (c. Dynasty 20) and commentary. It was discovered in KV 9.

84. Slightly modified from Faulkner, *Cambridge Ancient History* II, Part II, 240ff.

85. Drenkhahn, *Die Elephantine-Stele*, 68ff.

86. Drenkhahn, *Die Elephantine-Stele*, 32.

87. M. Boraik, "Re-writing Egypt's History: The Stela of Bakenkhonsu," *Ancient Egypt* (December 2008/2009): 24–27. Importantly, the stela reveals that King Sethnakht was still ruling in Year 4—his highest date yet known (p. 25). See, for a contradictory point of view, A. V. Safronov, "A Stele of the High Priest of Amun Bakenkhonsu," *Vestnik drevnei' istorii* 4 (2009): 301–304.

CHAPTER 3

1. I would like to thank my colleagues Dorothea Arnold, Marsha Hill, Diana Craig Patch, Nicholas Reeves, Ann Macy Roth, Christine Lilyquist, and Isabel Stuenkel with whom I have discussed various aspects of this paper and whose comments and suggestions have been very helpful. My thanks also go to Gustavo Camps and Scott Murphy who provided the illustrations.

The first queen who appears to have been regent for her son is Merneith, mother of Den (c. 3013–2999 BCE), Toby A. H. Wilkinson, *Early Dynastic Egypt* (London: Routledge, 1999), 74–75.

2. For a discussion of women who wielded royal power in ancient Egypt, see Ann Macy Roth, "Models of Authority: Hatshepsut's Predecessors in Power," in *Hatshepsut: From Queen to Pharaoh*, ed. Catharine H. Roehrig et al. (New York: Metropolitan Museum of Art, 2005), 9–14. For an in-depth discussion of the functions of the king's mother, see Silke Roth, *Die Königsmutter des alten Ägypten von der Frühzeit biss zum Ende der 12. Dynastie*, Ägypten und Altes Testament 46 (Wiesbaden: Otto Harassowitz, 2001).

3. Richard A. Fazzini, James F. Romano, and Madeleine E. Cody, *Art for Eternity: Masterworks from Ancient Egypt* (London: Scala, 1999), cat. no. 15, 54–55.

4. The 18th-Dynasty name for this cemetery was simply The Great Place (*t3 st 't*), and it included the tombs of kings (where sometimes family members were buried), queens, and non-royal men and women who were close to the royal family.

5. For a discussion of the 18th-Dynasty queen's tombs in the Valley of the Kings, see Catharine H. Roehrig, "Some Thoughts on Queens' Tombs in the Valley of the Kings," in *Thebes and Beyond: Studies in Honor of Kent R. Weeks*, ed. Z. Hawass and S. Ikram, Supplément aux *Annales du Service des antiquités de l'Egypte* 41 (Cairo: Supreme Council of Antiquities, 2010), 181–196.

6. For queen's tomb plans, see Elizabeth Thomas, *The Royal Necropoleis of Thebes* (Princeton: privately published, 1966), 200, 215; Bertha Porter and Rosalind Moss, *Topographical Bibliography of Ancient Egyptian Hieroglyphic Texts, Reliefs, and Paintings. The Theban Necropolis: Royal Tombs and Smaller Cemeteries*, Vol. 2:1 (Oxford: Clarendon Press, 1964), 750, 760.

7. Hartwig Altenmüller, "Der Begräbnistag Sethos' II," *Studien our Altägyptischen Kultur* 10 (1984): 38, and in Chapter 4 of this volume. Although neither graffito on which this suggestion is based has a king's name, I agree with Altenmüller's reasoning. There is no evidence to suggest that a tomb was ever begun for Tausret in the Valley of the Queens, where one would expect to find the tomb of a king's principal wife of this period.

8. Although the Egyptian civil calendar allowed for 365 days in the year, the Egyptians never calculated the need for a leap year. In time, the actual seasons (*akhet*—

inundation or flood season, *peret*—growing or winter season, and *shemu*—harvest or summer season) became disconnected from the civil calendar.

9. Even Nefertari, the favorite wife of Ramesses II, was not accorded this privilege, though she was given an exquisite tomb of her own in the Valley of the Queens.

10. Tausret's tomb also has little in common with 18th-Dynasty queens' tombs. In any case, these earlier queens' tombs were all excavated with steep entrances that were intended to be hidden after their final use and none would have been visible in the time of Sety II and Tausret.

11. As with all Ramesside king's tombs after Merenptah, KV 14 has a shallower drop in elevation than earlier kings' tombs in the Valley. Although chamber F in KV 14 (E on the plan, Figure 4.1) has no pillars, in all other respects it mimics the pillared hall. The well chamber is not excavated in Tausret's tomb, but neither are those in many of the later Ramesside tombs, including that of Tausret's husband, Sety II (KV 15).

12. This type of burial chamber is first used in the tomb of Ramesses II (KV 8). The tombs of this king's mother (QV 80) and his principal wife, Nefertari (QV 66), have truncated versions of this burial chamber with only four pillars and no vault.

13. First published by J. von Beckerath, "Queen Twosre as Guardian of Siptah," *Journal of Egyptian Archaeology* 48 (1962): 70–74. For other photographs of this piece, see Alfred Grimm and Sylvia Schoske, *Hatschepsut: Königin Ägyptens* (Munich: Staatliche Sammlung Ägyptischer Kunst, 1999), 61, cat. # 24; Christiane Ziegler, *Queens of Egypt from Hetepheres to Cleopatra* (Paris: Somogy, 2008), 370, cat. #219.

14. In general, deities do not wear sandals.

15. In her monograph *Die Elephantine-Stele des Sethnacht und ihr historischer Hintergrund* (Wiesbaden: Otto Harrassowitz, 1980), 35–38, Rosemarie Drenkhahn makes a case for the adult in this statue being Bay, and the viciousness of the attack on the adult does seem more appropriate for Bay, who was put to death by Siptah. However, the adult is seated on a standard royal throne, and this is more in keeping with its being Tausret. In 18th-Dynasty representations of non-royal nurses and tutors holding royal children (and in three cases the king) on their laps, the chair or stool of the nurse/tutor is not decorated with royal insignia; see Catharine H. Roehrig, *The Eighteenth Dynasty Titles Royal Nurse(mn't nswt), Royal Tutor (mn' nswt), and Foster Brother/Sister of the Lord of the Two Lands (sn/snt mn' n nb t3wy)*, Ph.D. dissertation, 1990 (UMI Dissertation Services, 9103856), 271–307.

16. Henri Gauthier, *Le Temple d'Amada* (Cairo: Institut Français d'Archéologie orientale, 1913), 108–109, pl. XX–XXI.

17. One exception is the tomb of Thutmose III (KV 34) where his principal queen, Merytre Hatshepsut, appears twice as a small figure in the context of the Amduat texts on the walls and once on a pillar with the king and other female members of his family.

18. In general, when a woman of any rank has a tomb or tomb chapel of her own, her husband does not appear in the decoration. This is a tradition that dates from the Old Kingdom; see Ann Macy Roth, "The Absent Spouse: Patterns and Taboos in Egyptian Tomb Decoration," *Journal of the American Research Center in Egypt* 36 (1999): 37–53.

19. For example, in the Valley of the Queens tombs of Khaemwas (QV 44) and Amenherkhepeshef (QV 55), both sons of Ramesses III.

20. The daughter-wives of Ramesses II, Meritamun, and Bintanat wear a similar hairstyle when they are depicted on colossal statues of their father in Luxor Temple.

21. This would be chamber J1, following Elizabeth Thomas and the Theban Mapping Project.

22. Hassan S. K. Bakry, "The Discovery of a Statue of Queen Twosre (1202–1194 BCE) at Madinet Nasr, Cairo," *Rivista degli Studi Orientali* 46 (1971): 17–26, pls. I–VIII.

23. The seated figure is about 110 cm (43 ¼ in) high at the shoulders, which would be life size for a woman of five foot four to six inches in height. This might be slightly over life size for an ancient Egyptian woman.

24. For the complete text, see Bakry, "The Discovery," pls. IV–VIII.

25. For example, the principal wife of Ramesses II is called Nefertari-beloved-of-Mut.

26. The stela is translated in Kenneth A. Kitchen, *Ramesside Inscriptions, Translated and Annotated, Translations*, vol. IV, *Merenptah and the Late Nineteenth Dynasty, Notes and Comments* (Oxford: Blackwell, 2003), #127, 216–218.

27. On page 1 of his text, Hassan calls this sandstone and says that the stone came from the quarries at Gebel Ahmar. This quarry is principally noted for its quartzite as Hassan later states on p. 25. I am, thus, assuming that this statue is made of quartzite.

28. Drovetti Collection. Black granite, inv. no. 1380, h. 194 cm. See Anna Maria Donadoni Roveeri, ed., *Egyptian Civilization:Monumental Art* (Milan: Electra, 1989), 158, fig. 244.

29. Georges Legrain, *Statues et Statuettes de Rois et de Particuliers, Catalogue Générale des Antiquités Égyptiennes du Musée du Caire*, vol. 49 (Cairo: IFAO Press, 1906).

30. The seated statue of Ramesses in Turin also holds only the crook.

31. For example, a fragmentary statue of Sety I in Vienna (Inv.-Nr. ÄS 5910) holds only the crook, whereas Siptah holds both the crook and flail in the Munich statue mentioned above. A seated statue of Akhenaten in the Louvre (N 831) also holds both crook and flail.

32. H. J. Franken, "The Excavations at Deir 'Alla in Jordan: 2nd Season," *Vetus Testamentum* 11:4 (October 1961): 365, with a drawing (pl. 4b), and a photograph (pl. 5).

33. Jean Yoyotte, "Un souvenir du 'pharaon' Taousert en Jordanie," *Vetus Testamentum* 12:4 (October 1962): 464–469. This reading was later published by Franken in the final publication of the site; see H. J. Franken, *Excavations at Deir 'Allā: The Late Bronze Age Sanctuary* (Louvain: Peters Press, 1992), 30–31, fig. 3–9.

34. Marcel Marée, "A Jar from Sidon with the Name of Pharaoh-Queen Tausret," *Archaeology & History in the Lebanon* 24 (Winter 2006): 121–128.

35. Yoyotte, "Un souvenir," 166–167.

36. Legrain, *Statues et Statuettes*, vol. I, CG 42123, 42125, 42126 from the mid-18th Dynasty have a cartouche of the king on the right shoulder and the right chest; vol. II, 42174 has the throne name of Ramesses II on the right shoulder.

37. G. A. Gaballa, "Some Nineteenth Dynasty Monuments in Cairo Museum," *Bulletin de l'Institut Français d'Archéologie Orientale* 71 (1972): 134.

38. This would be corridor L following Elizabeth Thomas and the Theban Mapping Project.

39. This would be chamber J2 following Elizabeth Thomas and the Theban Mapping Project.

40. This would be corridor K2 following Elizabeth Thomas and the Theban Mapping Project.

41. Tausret's husband, Sety II, died before his tomb could be completed (see Inset Box in chapter 3), so it is quite a bit shorter in length that of the other kings mentioned.

42. That is to say after the first pillared hall (E on figure 4.1, this would be chamber F following Elizabeth Thomas and the Theban Mapping Project), which in Tausret's tomb has no pillars.

43. It is true that Hatshepsut appears to have reburied her father, Thutmose I, in her own tomb—but this event took place some 250 years before Tausret's time, and Thutmose I was reburied a second time by his grandson, Thutmose III. Although there may have been some vague memory of these happenings a dozen generations later, it seems unlikely that this would have influenced Tausret to do something similar.

44. Lana Troy, *Patterns of Queenship in Ancient Egyptian Myth and History* (Upsala: Acta Universitatis Upsaliensis, 1986), 68–72 and elsewhere. For a summary of the iconography that suggests a notion of divine queenship, see Gay Robins, *Women in Ancient Egypt* (Cambridge, MA: Harvard University Press, 1993), 23–25.

45. Hartwig Altenmüller, "Dritter Vorbericht über die Arbeiten des Archäologischen Instituts der Universität Hamburg am Grab des Bay (KV 13) im Tal der Königs von Theben," *Studien zur Altägyptischen Kultur* 21 (1994): 4–7.

46. For drawings of three of these, see H. Altenmüller, "Bemerkungen zu den Königsgräbern des Neuen Reiches," *Studien zur Altägyptischen Kultur* 10 (1983): abb. 2 on p. 47.

47. It is possible that she would have made a larger outer sarcophagus in which her queen's sarcophagus could have been placed—but it would have to have been larger than either of the ones now inscribed for Siptah or Sethnakht.

48. Theodore M. Davis et al.,eds., *The Tomb of Siphtah: The Monkey Tomb and the Gold Tomb* (London: Archibald Constable, 1908).

49. George Daressy, "Catalogue of Jewels and Precious Objects Found in the Funerary Deposit of Setuî and Tauosrît," in *The Tomb of Siphtah*, ed. T. M. Davis et al., 43.

50. Some of these beads are now in the Egyptian Museum, Cairo (CG 52679), and others, which went to Davis in the division of finds, are in the Metropolitan Museum of Art, New York (30.8.66). Presumably these were once part of a single necklace. Several other beads from this necklace were found by the Amarna Royal Tombs Project in their 2002 season and are stored with the expedition finds in the SCA magazine at Qurna; see Nicholas Reeves and Geoffrey T. Martin, "ARTP's 4th season of work, 2002: where we dug and what we found," http://www.nicholasreeves.com/item.aspx?category=Writing&id=101 (accessed 2/11).

51. For example, the 12th-Dynasty jewelry of the King's Daughter Sithathoryunet is inscribed with the names of her male relatives Senwosret II and Amenemhat III while her name and title are only recorded on the four canopic jars from her tomb. The 18th-Dynasty jewelry of the three foreign wives of Thutmose III is inscribed with his name while their names are known only from canopic jars and heart scarabs.

52. G. Maspero, "King Siptah and Queen Tauosrît," in *The Tomb of Siphtah*, ed. T. M. Davis et al., xxviii; E. R. Ayrton, "The Unnamed Gold Tomb," in *The Tomb of Siphtah*, ed. T. M. Davis et al., 32.

53. Cyril Aldred, "Valley Tomb no. 56 at Thebes," *Journal of Egyptian Archaeology* 49 (1963): 177. Reeves and Martin, "ARTP's 4th season of work, 2002," however, have suggested that there was perhaps an original queen's burial from the late 18th Dynasty.

54. Davis et al., eds., *The Tomb of Siphtah*, 4.

55. Davis et al., eds., *The Tomb of Siphtah*, 31–32.

56. Personal communication from Nicholas Reeves and Paul Sussman, December 2010.

57. The king's daughter Sithathoryunet was buried with jewelry inscribed with the names of two different kings, one probably her father and the second perhaps a nephew, suggesting that the jewelry had a ceremonial or magical value that continued after a king's death.

CHAPTER 4

1. R. Pococke, *A Description of the East, and Some other Countries*, Vol. 1 (London: W. Boyer, 1743), pl. XXXII (G) facing p. 99. On Pococke's overview map (p. 97), the tomb of Queen Tausret is labeled with the letter "H."

2. *Description de l'Egypte ou Recueil des observations et des recherches qui ont été faites en Egypte pendant l'expédition de l'armée française publiée sous les ordres de Napoléon Bonaparte*, Vol. II, 1st ed. (Paris: 1818), pl. 78.

3. L. Costaz, *Description de l'Egypte ou Recueil des observations et des recherches qui ont été faites en Egypte pendant l'expédition de l'armée française*. Seconde édition, Vol. III, 2nd ed. Antiquités—descriptions (Paris: Charles Louis Fleury Panckoucke, 1821), 210–214.

4. J. F. Champollion, *Monuments de l'Égypte et de la Nubie: Notices descriptives conformes aux manuscrits autographes rédigés sur les lieux par Champollion le Jeune*, Vol. 1 (Paris, Firmin Didot frères, 1844), 448–459; 806–808.

5. R. Lepsius, *Denkmäler aus Ägypten und Äthiopien: nach den Zeichnungen der von Seiner Majestät dem Könige von Preussen Friedrich Wilhelm IV. nach diesen Ländern gesendeten und in den Jahren 1842–1845 ausgeführten wissenschaftlichen Expedition*, vol. III (Berlin: Nicolaische Buchhandlung, 1849–1859), pl. 201a–b; 205; 206a–c; R. Lepsius, *Denkmäler: Text*, Vol. 3 (Leipzig: Eduard Naville, 1900), 209–214.

6. A. H. Gardiner, "Only One King Siptah and Twosre Not His Wife," *Journal of Egyptian Archaeology* 44 (London, 1958): 12–22.

7. H. H. Nelson, *Medinet Habu*, Vol. IV, *Festival Scenes of Ramses III*, OIP 51 (Chicago: Oriental Institute Press, 1940), pl. 207 and pl. 203.

8. http://www.thebanmappingproject.com/.

9. The project is funded by the German Research Foundation (Deutsche Forschungsgemeinschaft), Bonn. Members of the Tausret-Project (Tausret-Projekt) were Hartwig Altenmüller (director), Friedrich Abitz (co-director), Hans Ballschuh (photography), Jan Lindemann (graphics), Christiane Preuss-Altenmüller (graphics), Elke Roik (architecture), Bernd Scheel (graphics), Abdelghaffar Shedid (photography). Members of the Bay-Project and who recorded the sarcophagus were Hartwig Altenmüller (director), Ute Effland (graphics), Kosmas Karoly (photography), Ute Rummel (graphics).

10. oCairo J. 72452; K. A. Kitchen, *Ramesside Inscriptions, Historical and Biographical*, Vol. IV (Oxford: Blackwell, 1982), 404; A. H. Gardiner, "Only One King Siptah and Twosre Not His Wife," 19; *Journal of Egyptian Archaeology* 44 (1958): 19; W. Helck, "Drei Ramessidische Daten," *Studien zur Altägyptischen Kultur* 17 (1990): 208–210.

11. A. H. Gardiner, "The Tomb of Queen Twosre," *Journal of Egyptian Archaeology* 40 (1954): 43 n. 3; K. A. Kitchen, *Ramesside Inscriptions, Translated and Annotated, Translations, vol. IV, Merenptah and the Late Nineteenth Dynasty* (Oxford: Blackwell, 2003), 289.

12. Helck, "Drei Ramessidische Daten," 208–210; H. Altenmüller, Bemerkungen zu den neu gefundenen Daten im Grab der Königin Twosre (KV 14) im Tal der Könige von Theben, in *After Tutcankhamun. Research and Excavation in the Royal Necropolis at Thebes, Studies in Egyptology*, ed. C. N. Reeves (London: Kegan Paul International, 1992), 147–151; oCairo CG 25521 rt. (Kitchen, *Ram. Inscr.*, IV, 397); oCairo CG 25521 vs (Kitchen, *Ram. Inscr.*, IV, 400); oCairo CG 25536 (Kitchen, *Ram. Inscr.*, IV, 402).

13. H. Altenmüller, "Der Begräbnistag Sethos II," *Studien zur Altägyptischen Kultur* 11 (1984): 37–47; H. Altenmüller, "Das Graffito 551 aus der Thebanischen Nekropole," *Studien zur Altägyptischen Kultur* 21 (1994): 19–28.

14. The designations of the rooms are taken from B. Porter and R. L. B. Moss, *Topographical Bibliography of Ancient Egyptian Hieroglyphic Texts, Reliefs, and Paintings. I. The Theban Necropolis. Part 2. Royal Tombs and Smaller Cemeteries*, 2nd ed. (Oxford: Clarendon Press, 1964), 527–532.

15. Costaz, *Description de l'Egypte*, Vol. III, 210. "On trouvre deux grandes salles sépucrales semblables à la salle principale du tombeau des harpes."

16. Lepsius, *Denkmäler, Text*, Vol. III, 214; Gardiner, "The Tomb of Queen Twosre," 44. More references in Altenmüller, "Bemerkungen zu den neu gefundenen Daten," 162 n. 6.

17. Altenmüller, "Bemerkungen zu den neu gefundenen Daten," pp. 142–145.

18. The cartouches read: Lord of the Two Lands Satre-Meritamun Lord of appearances Tausret Setepetenmut. (*nb(t) t3wj (S3t-R⁽ mrjjt-Jmn), nb(t) ḫ⁽w (T3-wsrt stpt-n-Mwt)*).

19. F. Abitz, "Zur Bedeutung der beiden Nebenräume hinter der Sarkophaghalle der Königin Tausret," *Studien zur Altägyptischen Kultur* 9 (1981): 1–8.

20. Altenmüller, "Bemerkungen zu den neu gefundenen Daten," 152–154. If Siptah had died in this year, his day of death would have been in the second month of the inundation season of the 6th [regnal] year.

21. The 6th regnal year for Siptah is listed in a graffito from Buhen (Kitchen, *Ram. Inscr.*, IV, 365,4) meaning Siptah's death could not have happened before the sixth regnal year. Siptah's sixth regnal year began in the first month of the Peret season. The date from the second month of the inundation from K1a/K1b must therefore refer to the tenth month of the sixth regnal year. This corresponds to oKairo CG 25792 (Kitchen, *Ram. Inscr.*, IV, 414), which names a royal burial day on the twenty-second day of the fourth month of inundation (= 22. IV.); this day usually occurred seventy days after the day of death because of the necessary preparations; thus the king in question could have died on the thirteenth of the second month of the inundation (= 13. II.). Until now this date was thought to have been the day of Siptah's burial and was placed on the twenty-second day of the fourth month of the inundation in the sixth regnal year of Siptah/Tausret. Because of the indication in Pap. Greg, which reports that on the twenty-second day of the fourth month of the inundation of the sixth regnal year of Siptah/Tausret, construction was going on in the Valley of the Kings, W. Helck ("Die Datierung des Papyrus Greg," in *Gedenkschrift für Winfried Barta*, ḥtp dj n ḥzj, ed. D.

Kessler and R. Schulz , Münchner Ägyptologische Untersuchungen [Frankfurt: Peter Lang, 1995], 203) assumed that the date of the burial was in the seventh regnal year, and not the sixth. One condition for this is the assumption that work stopped on the day of a burial in the Valley of the Kings. This assumption is unproven. It has been verified that the men working on Tausret's tomb were in the Valley of the Kings during Sety II's burial, undoubtedly to work (cf. note 13 above). For this reason, I still think it is possible that the ostracon lists the burial day of Siptah in the sixth year, whereby the real date of Tausret's ascension to the throne must have been sometime around the thirteenth of the second month of the inundation of the sixth year of Tausret and that in effect the date in K1a/K1b refers to a change in plan marking her ascension to the throne.

22. The reveals of all of the doorways were cut back by 0.15–0.18 meter (.49–.59 feet), so that the width increased from 1.53 meters (5.01 feet) to 1.68/1.71 meters (5.51/5.61feet).

23. The measurements are length 3.25 meters (10.66 feet), width 1.62 meters (5.31 feet), height 2.59 meters (8.49 feet).

24. If the sarcophagus of Mentuherchopeschef, which was found in the tomb of Bay (KV 13), really is the original royal sarcophagus of Tausret, no new work was necessary. The measurements of the sarcophagus are length 3.20 meters (10.49 feet), width 1.40/1.45 meters (4.59/4.75 feet), height 2.08/2.20 meters (6.82/7.21 feet).

25. In the entryway and in corridors B, C, H, and K2.

26. It is not the rediscovered sarcophagus of the "Great Royal Wife" Tausret that was found in the neighboring tomb of Bay (KV 13) and was reused for prince Amunherchopeschef, but a much larger sarcophagus, which was also found in the tomb of Bay and which was left in an unfinished state by Tausret. This sarcophagus later was reworked for prince Mentuherchopeschef, probably during the reign of Ramesses III.

27. In the tomb of Merenptah (KV 8), the cut away doorways were replaced after a similar procedure. This is still visible: E. C. Brock, "The Tomb of Merenptah and Its Sarcophagi," in *After Tutankhamun. Research and Excavation in the Royal Necropolis at Thebes*, ed. C. N. Reeves, Studies in Egyptology (London: Kegan Paul International, 1992), 122–140.

28. Usually the collision of KV 10 and KV 11 and the unfinished state of KV 11 are given as the reasons for choosing KV 14; cf. E. Thomas, *The Royal Necropoleis of Thebes* (Princeton: privately published, 1966), 125; J. Černý, *The Valley of the Kings. Fragments d'un manuscrit inachevé*, Bibliothèque d'étude 61 (Cairo: Institut Français d'Archéologie Orientale du Caire, 1973), 9; R. Drenkhahn, *Die Elephantine-Stele des Sethnacht und ihr historischer Hintergrund*, Ägyptologische Abhandlungen 36 (Wiesbaden: Harrassowitz, 1980), 58–59. The cited reasons are only partially convincing. See Altenmüller, "Bemerkungen zu den neu gefundenen Daten," 142–143. Other possible reasons are discussed later in the chapter.

29. Gardiner, "The Tomb of Queen Twosre," 41. A. H. Gardiner lists a number of convincing arguments for dating the decoration in the first corridor to the time of Siptah.

30. Lepsius, *Denkmäler*, Text III, 213; Gardiner, "The Tomb of Queen Twosre," 42.

31. H. Altenmüller, "Das Grab der Königin Tausret im Tal der Könige von Theben," *Studien zur Altägyptischen Kultur* 10 (1983), 16–18; Altenmüller, "Bemerkungen zu den neu gefundenen Daten im Grab der Königin Twosre," 160–162; H. Altenmüller, "Tausrets Weg zum Königtum," in *Das Königtum der Ramessidenzeit. Voraussetzungen—*

Verwirklichung—Vermächtnis, ed. R. Gundlach and U. Rößler-Köhler, Ägypten und Altes Testament 36,3 (Wiesbaden: Harrassowitz, 2003), 114; H. Altenmüller, "A Biography in Stone," in *Queens of Egypt from Hetepheres to Cleopatra,* ed. C. Ziegler (Monaco: Somogy Editions d'Art, 2008), 208.

32. Ziegler, *Queens of Egypt from Hetepheres to Cleopatra,* 296, 313 (Cat. Nr. 139) and passim.

33. The inscriptions are designed in the infinitive as texts to the scenes. The offering scenes in the first corridor (A) are in sunk relief, which indicates an earlier version. They can only be found on the northern wall of the first corridor, that is, the offering to Ptah and Maat (A-N/1), the king offering incense and water to Geb in combination with the queen offering ointment (A-N/2), and a wine offering to Re-Horakhty (A-N/3).

34. The texts of the inscriptions can be found in F. Abitz, *König und Gott. Die Götterszenen in den ägyptischen Königsgräbern von Thutmosis IV. bis Ramses III.,* Ägyptologische Abhandlungen 40 (Wiesbaden: Harrassowitz, 1984), 282–283, No. 266–272.

35. Altenmüller, "Das Grab der Königin Tausret im Tal der Könige," 16–20; Altenmüller, "Bemerkungen zu den neu gefundenen Daten," 155–157; Altenmüller, "Tausrets Weg zum Königtum," 126 fig. 5.

36. The inscription with her titulary reads: "Osiris, Great Royal Wife, lord/mistress of the Two Lands, Tausret, may she live in eternity."

37. The hieroglyphs of the name/titulary are partially overlapped by the blue crown of the third version. The cartouches read *nb t3wj* ([*S3t-R^c*] *hnwt T3-mrj*) *nb h^cw* (*T3-wsrt* [*3ht n*] *Mwt*).

38. As can be seen in corridor A in scenes A-S/1, A-S/4; A-N/3. Also in the other corridors, there are signs of the lowered hand.

39. The cartouches contain, as one now knows, the so-called late version of the name. At the beginning of his reign, Siptah has the names *Sh^c-n-R^c stp-n-R^c* and *R^c-ms-sw S3-Pth,* which replace the names attested in scene *3-š/3 3h-n-R^c stp-n-R^c ^cnd Mrj-n-Pth S3-Pth.* The change in names is documented for the first time in year 3 of Siptah and must therefore have occurred between the king's first and third year: Gardiner, "Only One King Siptah," 12–14; Drenkhahn, *Die Elephantine-Stele des Sethnacht,* 5.

40. Gardiner, "Only One King Siptah," 12–14.

41. Irrespective of the fact that construction on the tomb began in the second regnal year of Sety II, as stated in oCairo J 72452.

42. It is unknown if the names of Siptah had been replaced by those of Sety II.

43. Good examples for the sequence of images are in Z. Hawass and S. Vannini, *Bilder der Unsterblichkeit. Die Totenbücher aus den Königsgräbern in Theben* (Mainz: Philipp von Zabern, 2006), 246–249 (fold-out plate).

44. An illustration of the scenes in H. Altenmüller, "Die Wandlungen des Sem-Priesters im Mundöffnungsritual," *Studien zur Altägyptischen Kultur* 38 (2009): 29–32.

45. In the doorway to chamber G, in the scenes of purifying with Upper Egyptian incense (scenes 4b and 4c of the Opening of the Mouth ceremony), the name of the ruling queen can be found in two places above the cartouche of the "Great Royal Wife"; another revision is in scene 6 at the beginning of the purification with incense (scene 6c). The revision in scene 12e is less obvious.

46. An illustration in Abitz, *König und Gott,* 76–79, figs. 32–34; the accompanying texts on pp. 282–283, No. 266–272.

47. On the walls of the antechambers of the burial chamber of Merenptah (KV 8) and Ramesses III (KV 11) are comparable images and texts from the judgment of the dead: Abitz, *König und Gott*, 41 and 82 with reference to Champollion, *Notices descriptives*, 418.

48. Images in burial chamber J can be found in A. De Luca and K. R. Weeks, eds., *Im Tal der Könige. Von Grabkunst und Totenkult der ägyptischen Herrscher* (Augsburg: Weltbild, 2001), 226–231; Hawass and Vannini, *Bilder der Unsterblichkeit*, 183–184.

49. H. Altenmüller, "Dritter Vorbericht über die Arbeiten des Archäologischen Instituts am Grab des Bay (KV 13) im Tal der Könige von Theben," *Studien zur Altägyptischen Kultur* 21 (1994), 5, fig. 2; Altenmüller, "A Biography in Stone," 214 fig. 80; H. Altenmüller, "Prinz und Pharao. Amunherchopeschef und Ramses VI," in *Die ihr vorbeigehen werdet... Wenn Gräber, Tempel und Statuen sprechen, Gedenkschrift für Prof. Dr. Sayed Tawfik Ahmed*, ed. U. Rößler-Köhler and T. Tawfik. Sonderschriften Deutsches Archäologisches Institut Kairo 16 (Berlin: Walter de Gruyter, 2009), 9–12, pl. 4.

50. See footnote 18.

51. E. Hornung, *Das Amduat. Die Schrift des verborgenen Raumes, Teil I: Text; Teil II Übersetzung und Kommentar*, Ägyptologische Abhandlungen 7 (Wiesbaden: Harrassowitz, 1963), 123.

52. Such a procedure is indicated by the beam holes in K2, in which beams were mounted that were not only used for bringing in the sarcophagus but also for removing it.

53. The sarcophagus for Tausret in her role as pharaoh could be the one reused for Mentuherkhopeschef from corridor H of the tomb of Bay (KV 13): Altenmüller, "Prinz und Pharao," 7–9, pl. 4–5. In this essay, the identification with Mentuherkhopeschef, son of Ramesses VI, has to be revised under these circumstances and the named Mentuherkhopeschef must be connected with a son of Ramesses III and not a son of Ramesses VI, as I previously assumed. Cf. H. Altenmüller, "Prinz Mentu-her-chopeschef aus der 20. Dynastie," *Mitteilungen des Deutschen Archäologischen Instituts, Abteilung Kairo* 50 (1994): 1–12.

54. Cf. note 24 above.

55. Papyrus Harris I, 75.4; C. Maderna-Sieben, "Der historische Abschnitt des Papyrus Harris I," *Göttinger Miszellen* 123 (1991): 61; P. Grandet, *Le Papyrus Harris I* (BM 9999), Vol. I–II, Bibliothèque d'étude 109:1–2 (Cairo: Institut Français d'Archéologie Orientale du Caire, 1994), vol. 2, 220 n. 901.

CHAPTER 5

1. For the most recent study of these temples, see Christian Leblanc, ed., *The Temples of Millions of Years: Science and New Technologies Applied to Archaeology*, Acts of the International Symposium, Luxor, January 2010 (Cairo: Supreme Council of Antiquities, 2011).

2. See Martina Ullmann, *König für die Ewigkeit: die Häuser der Millionen von Jahre: eine Untersuchung zu Königskult und Tempeltypologie in Ägypten*, ÄAT 51 (Wiesbaden: Harrassowitz, 2002).

3. W. M. Flinders Petrie, *Six Temples at Thebes* (London: Bernard Quaritch, 1897), 13. All subsequently published plans of this temple, until those of our own expedition, have been based on Petrie's plan. See, for example, U. Holscher, *The Mortuary Temple of Ramesses III*, Part I, Vol. III of *The Excavation of Medinet Habu*, University of Chicago Oriental Institute Publication LIV (Chicago: University of Chicago, 1941), 22–32.

4. Petrie did not deny that the temple might have been completed, and his published account is ambiguous on this point: "Of the building of the temple only a few stones of the foundation remained…otherwise the only evidences of it were the foundation trenches cut in the gravel and marl ground" (*Six Temples*, p. 13). But his findings have been universally understood to show that the temple was only begun and never completed. This understanding may be seen in recent publications referring to the site, and even those discussing Petrie's work there. So, for example, the summary of Petrie's work at the Tausret site on the website of University College London (accessed in November 2011) concludes, "It can be assumed that the building was never finished and already stopped at an early state of construction" (http://www.digitalegypt.ucl. ac.uk/thebes/tausret/index.html).

5. The staff of the University of Arizona Egyptian Expedition is made up of Egyptologists, supporting specialists, and advanced students from several universities in North America and elsewhere. Current staff members who have worked on the Tausret Temple Project include Expedition Director Dr. Richard Wilkinson (University of Arizona), Dr. Karin Kroenke, Dr. Teresa Moore (University of California, Berkeley), Dr. Mary Ownby (Cambridge University), Dr. Ahmed Fahmy (Helwan University), Dr. Robert Demarée (Leiden University), Dr. Suzanne Onstine (University of Memphis), Omar Abu Zaid (Sohag University), Dr. Pearce Paul Creasman, Aaryn Brewer, Adam Cirzan, Linda Gosner, Damian Greenwell, Danielle Phelps, Dr. Gonzalo Sanchez, Christopher Schafer, Mark Wilkinson (University of Arizona), Richard Harwood (Colorado), Donald Kunz (Arizona), Stephanie Denkowicz (New York), Ashleigh Goodwin (University of Liverpool), Lyla Brock, Rexine Hummel (Royal Ontario Museum). The assistance of other staff members who have worked with the Expedition at various times since its inception is acknowledged in our formal reports and publications.

6. The author would like to thank the members of the Permanent Committee of the Supreme Council of Antiquities for granting us permission to initiate and to continue this project, and Dr. Mohamed Ismael, Director of Foreign Missions, for his continued help in arranging our work in Egypt. In Luxor, the Director of Upper Egyptian Antiquities, Mr. Mansour Boraik, has been a great help—as always—and we thank him particularly. We also thank Mr. Ali El-Asfar, who was Director of West Bank Antiquities during our 2004–2009 seasons, and Mr. Mustafa El-Waziry who took over that office in 2009. Mr. Mohamed Hamdan, Director of the West Bank Missions Office, has been extremely helpful, and we also thank all our assigned local inspectors who have been a great help. Reis Ali Farouk Sayed El-Quftawi, Reis Omar Farouk Sayed El-Quftawi, and Assistant Reis Kamal Helmy have all been of inestimable help to us. Our thanks are also due to the American Research Center in Egypt which has facilitated our Expedition during the course of this project—and most especially to Mme. Amira Khattab, whose constantly kind and able help we greatly appreciate.

7. These field seasons would not have been possible without the generous help of the individuals and institutions who have supported our work. We especially thank Stephanie Denkowicz, Mahmut Dogan, Donald and Edith Kunz, Kathryn Michel, Dr. Bonnie Sampsel, Ted Snook, the Amarna Research Foundation, and the American Research Center in Egypt.

8. Reports on our field seasons have been published in *The Ostracon: Journal of the Egyptian Study Society; Bulletin of the American Research Center in Egypt;* and elsewhere.

See, for example, Richard H. Wilkinson, "Six Seasons at Thebes: The University of Arizona Tausert Temple Project," in *Thebes and Beyond: Studies in Honor of Kent R. Weeks,* ed. Z. Hawass and S. Ikram, *Supplément aux Annales du Service des antiquites de l'Egypte* 41 (Cairo: Institut français d'archéologie orientale du Caire, 2010), 219–237. A final site report, *The Temple of Tausret,* is planned for publication by the UAEE in early 2012.

9. Petrie, *Six Temples,* p. 13, states explicitly, "These trenches were all cleared." Our findings do not suggest that Petrie knowingly misrepresented his work on the site. It is possible, and perhaps likely, that Petrie was not present for much of the time that limited probing and excavation were conducted by his men. See, for example, Richard H. Wilkinson, "Excavation in the Time of V.S. Golenischev: W. M. F. Petrie's Work at the Tausert Memorial Temple," in *Ancient Egypt*: Volume II, *On the Occasion of the 150th Birthday Anniversary of Vladimir S. Golenischev* , ed. V. V. Solkin (Moscow: Association of Ancient Egypt Studies, 2006), 160–165; pls. 69–73.

10. Petrie is renowned for having collected even the smallest artifacts from the sites he excavated, but we have found literally thousands of small artifacts—amulets, beads, shabtis, pieces of statues and stelae, and others—throughout the obviously unexplored areas of the site.

11. Petrie, *Six Temples,* 2, states that he paid his men the same amounts that he paid antiquities dealers for artifacts, although, as he notes, this did not stop artifacts being stolen by some of the local workmen.

12. Dr. Robert J. Demarée is thanked for his translation of these texts.

13. Two ostraca from Deir el-Medina are dated to Tausret's eighth year: oIFAO DM 594 and oCairo CG25293. See Kenneth A. Kitchen, *Ramesside Inscriptions, Translated and Annotated, Translations,* Vol. IV, *Merenptah and the Late Nineteenth Dynasty* (Oxford: Blackwell, 2003), 407–408.

14. For example, small mud brick walls were built every couple of meters throughout the site's foundation trenches and seem to have been constructed to stabilize the bed of sand upon which the heavy foundation blocks were set. These walls are of such an unusual, if not unique, nature (we do not know of any like them in the other Theban royal temples) that Petrie would surely have commented on them in his report had he been aware of them. Other architectural features include the remains of buildings and chapels clearly unexcavated.

15. Petrie certainly understood the importance of accurate archaeological plans. In his seminal work *Methods and Aims in Archaeology* he noted that the main purposes of archaeological excavation were to draw up "plans and topographical information" about sites in addition to obtaining portable antiquities: W. M. F. Petrie, *Methods and Aims in Archaeology* (London: Macmillan, 1904), 33.

16. The term "phase" is used here in the general sense of a stage in the overall history of the Tausret temple site rather than in the broader archeological sense of a regional phase of related components.

17. See, for example, the reconstruction on the University College London site. Available at http://www.digitalegypt.ucl.ac.uk/thebes/tausret/index.html (accessed November 2011).

18. "North" and other cardinal points mentioned in this chapter are based on local north as utilized by the ancient Egyptians. Local north on the Tausert site lies at 40 degrees east of magnetic north.

19. Such reuse of building materials from earlier structures was commonplace in ancient Egypt. We have discovered only a very few bricks stamped with the cartouche of Tausret herself (mainly in areas around foundation deposits). Most of the seal-impressed mud bricks on the site bear the cartouches of Thutmose IV and Merenptah, and it is evident that these bricks were originally cannibalized from the earlier temples directly to the north and south of the site of the queen's monument.

20. K. A. Kitchen, *Ramesside Inscriptions: Historical and Biographical*, Vol. 4 (Oxford: Blackwell, 1968–1990), 376–377; M. Marciniak, *Les inscriptions hiératiques du temple de Thoutmosis III* (Warsaw: PWN-Editions scientifiques de Pologne, 1974), 59–61, nr. 3.

21. Petrie, *Six Temples*, 13.

22. It should also be noted that the objects found in the foundation pits made for the stone temple mention only Tausret, and that Siptah is not mentioned at all.

23. The basic similarity had been noted in the past—see, for example, U. Hölscher, *The Mortuary Temple of Ramesses III*, Part I, Vol. III of *The Excavation of Medinet Habu* (Chicago: University of Chicago Oriental Institute, 1941), 24. But a number of the precise similarities were obscured by Petrie's inaccurate plan, and by the fact that Tausret's temple was modeled on the *inner* part of the Ramesseum only.

24. The azimuth of the temple of Tausret is 132.5 degrees compared to 131.5 for the Ramesseum and 122.5 for the Temple of Merenptah. Mosalem Shaltout and Juan Belmonte, "On the Orientation of Ancient Egyptian Temples: Upper Egypt and Lower Nubia," *Journal of the History of Astronomy* 36 (2005): 273–297.

25. Petrie, *Six Temples*, 13.

26. Not only was the first court "which was here 75 × 50 cubits, just the same size as that of Merenptah," but also the overall area of the two temples was the same: Petrie, *Six Temples*, 13.

27. These smaller stones may well have been utilized in dual rows for the construction of the temple's walls.

28. This point was stressed by Dr. Horst Jaritz, who excavated the nearby memorial temple of Merenptah, in his comments made in response to a presentation on the temple of Tausret at the international conference, "The Temples of Millions of Years," organized by the Supreme Council of Antiquities and held at Luxor in January 2010. I am very grateful to Dr. Jaritz and also to Dr. Christian Leblanc and Dr. Angelo Sesana for their helpful comparative comments.

29. These features are clearest on specially obtained high-resolution satellite images, but some may be seen on relatively low-resolution images available on Internet sites such as Google Earth.

30. This number, consisting of adult and juvenile individuals, is based on the analysis of the human remains by Dr. Gonzalo Sanchez, the Expedition's medical expert.

31. In earlier publications we had dated initial artifacts from this area to the Third Intermediate Period based on some confusing and misidentified traits of certain finds. It is now clear that the intrusive burials are of Late Period origin.

AFTERWORD

1. A more detailed synopsis of the story and its characters as well as illustrations from various editions was written by Marie-Cécile Bruwier, "The Romance of the Mummy and the True Tahoser," in *Queens of Egypt from Hetepheres to Cleopatra*, ed. Christiane Ziegler (Monaco: Somogy Editions d'Art, 2008), 216–227. This exhibition catalogue is available in both French and English. An English translation of the novel may be found online at http://www.horrormasters.com/Text/a2849.pdf.

Bibliography

Abitz, Friedrich. *Die Religiöse Bedeutung der sogenannten Grabräuberschächte in den ägyptischen Königsgräbern der 18. bis 20. Dynastie.* Ägyptologische Abhandlungen, no. 26, Wiesbaden: Harassowitz, 1974.

——. "Zur Bedeutung der beiden Nebenräume hinter der Sarkophaghalle der Königin Tausert." *Studien zur Altägyptischen Kultur* 9 (1981): 1–8.

——. *König und Gott. Die Götterszenen in den ägyptischen Königsgräbern von Thutmosis IV. bis Ramses III.* Ägyptologische Abhandlungen, no. 40. Wiesbaden: Harassowitz, 1984.

Aldred, Cyril. "Valley Tomb no. 56 at Thebes." *Journal of Egyptian Archaeology* 49 (1963): 177.

Altenmüller, Hartwig. "Tausret und Sethnacht." *Journal of Egyptian Archaeology* 68 (1982): 107–115.

——. "Das Grab der Königen Tausert im Tal der Könige von Theben: Erster Vorbericht über die Arbeiten des Archäologischen Instituts der Universität Hamburg im Winter 1982/1983." *Studien zur Altägyptischen Kultur* 10 (1983): 1–24.

——. "Rolle und Bedeutung des Grabes des Königin Tausret im Königsgräbertal von Theben." *Bulletin de la Société d'Égyptologie Geneve* 8 (1983): 3–11.

——. "Der Begräbnistag Sethos' II." *Studien zur Altägyptischen Kultur* 11, Festschrift für Wolfgang Helck (1984): 37–47.

——. "Das Grab der Königin Tausret (KV14): Bericht uber eine archäologische Unternehmung." *Göttinger Miszellen* 84 (1985): 7–17.

——. "La tombe de la reine Taouser." *Dossiers d'archéologie* 149–150 (1990): 64–67.

——. "Bemerkungen zu den neu gefundenen Daten im Grab der Königin Twosre (KV 14) im Tal der Könige von Theben." In *After Tutankhamun: Research and Excavation in the Royal Necropolis at Thebes,* ed. Carl Nicholas Reeves, 141–164. Studies in Egyptology, London: Kegan Paul International, 1992.

_____. "Zweiter Vorbericht über die Arbeiten des Archäologischen Instituts am Grab des Bay (KV 13) im Tal der Könige von Theben." *Studien zur Altägyptischen Kultur* 19 (1992): 15–36.

_____. "Dritter Vorbericht über die Arbeiten des Archäologischen Instituts am Grab des Bay (KV 13) im Tal der Könige von Theben." *Studien zur Altägyptischen Kultur* 21 (1994): 1–18.

_____. "Das Graffito 551 aus der Thebanischen Nekropole." *Studien zur Altägyptischen Kultur* 21 (1994): 19–28.

_____. "Prinz Mentu-her-chopeschef aus der 20. Dynastie." *Mitteilungen des Deutschen Archäologischen Instituts, Abteilung Kairo* 50 (1994): 1–12.

_____. "The Tomb of Tausert and Setnakht." In *The Treasures of the Valley of the Kings: Tombs and Temples of the Theban West Bank in Luxor*, ed. Kent R. Weeks, 222–231. Vercelli: WhiteStar, 2001; Cairo: American University in Cairo Press, 2001.

_____. "Tausrets Weg zum Königtum." In *Das Königtum der Ramessidenzeit*, ed. R. Gundlach and U. Rößler-Köhler, 109–128. Ägypten und Altes Testament, no. 36:3, Wiesbaden: Harassowitz, 2003.

_____."A Biography in Stone." In *Queens of Egypt from Hetepheres to Cleopatra*, ed. Christiane Ziegler, 208–215. Monaco: Somogy Editions d'Art, 2008.

_____. "Die Wandlungen des Sem-Priesters im Mundöffnungsritual." *Studien zur Altägyptischen Kultur* 38 (2009): 1–32.

_____. "Prinz und Pharao. Amunherchopeschef und Ramses VI." In *Die ihr vorbeigehen werdet... Wenn Gräber, Tempel und Statuen sprechen, Gedenkschrift für Prof. Dr. Sayed Tawfik Ahmed*, ed. U. Rößler-Köhler and T. Tawfik, 5–16. Sonderschriften Deutsches Archäologisches Institut Kairo, no. 16. Berlin, New York: Walter de Gruyter, 2009.

Amélineau, Émile. *Les Nouvelles Fouilles D'Abydos 1895–1898*. Paris: Ernest Leroux, 1899.

Arnold, Dorothea. "Aspects of the Royal Female Image during the Amarna Period." In *The Royal Women of Amarna: Images of Beauty from Ancient Egypt*, ed. Dorothea Arnold, 85–119. New York: Metropolitan Museum of Art, 1996.

Ayrton, E. R. "The Unnamed Gold Tomb." In *The Tomb of Siphtah: The Monkey Tomb and the Gold Tomb*, ed. Theodore M. Davis, 31–34. London: A. Constable, 1908.

Bakry, H. S. K. "The Discovery of a Statue of Queen Twosre (1202–1194? B.C.) at Medinet Nasr, Cairo." *Revista Studi Orientali* 45 (1971): 17–26.

Beckereth, J. von. "Queen Twosre as Guardian of Siptah." *Journal of Egyptian Archaeology* 48 (1962): 69.

Blankenberg-Van Delden, C. *The Large Commemorative Scarabs of Amenhotep III*. Leiden: Brill, 1969.

_____. "More Large Commemorative Scarabs of Amenophis III." *Journal of Egyptian Archaeology* 62 (1976): 74–80.

Breasted, J. H. *Ancient Records of Egypt* Vol. III. Chicago: University of Chicago Press, 1906.

Brock, Edwin C. "The Tomb of Merenptah and Its Sarkophagi." In *After Tutᶜankhamun. Research and Excavation in the Royal Necropolis at Thebes*, ed. Carl Nicholas Reeves, 122–140. London: Kegan Paul International, 1992.

Bryan, Betsy M. *Mistress of the House, Mistress of Heaven: Women in Ancient Egypt*. New York: Hudson Hill Press, 1997.

Callender, Vivianne G. "Queen Tausret and the End of Dynasty 19." *Studien zur Altägyptischen Kultur* 32 (2004): 81–104.

___ (published as Gae Callender). "The Cripple, the Queen and the Man from the North." *KMT: A Modern Journal of Ancient Egypt* 17:1 (2006): 46–61.

Champollion, Jean François. *Monuments de l'Égypte et de la Nubie: Notices descriptives conformes aux manuscrits autographes rédigés sur les lieux par Champollion le Jeune.* 4 vols. Paris: Firmin Didot frères, 1835–1845.

Čérný, Jaroslav. "A Note on the Chancellor Bay." *Zeitschrift für Ägyptische Sprache und Altertumskunde* 93 (1966): 35–39.

___. *The Valley of the Kings. Fragments d'un manuscrit inachevé.* Bibliothèque d'étude, no. 61, Cairo: Institut Français d'Archéologie Orientale du Caire, 1973.

Daressy, George. "Catalogue of Jewels and Precious Objects Found in the Funerary Deposit of Setuî and Tauosrît." In *The Tomb of Siphtah: the Monkey Tomb and the Gold Tomb,* ed. Theodore M. Davis, 35–44. London: A. Constable, 1908.

Davis, Theodore M., ed. *The Tomb of Siphtah: The Monkey Tomb and the Gold Tomb.* London: A. Constable, 1908.

De Buck, Adrian. "The Judicial Papyrus of Turin." *Journal of Egyptian Archaeology* 23:2 (1937): 152–164.

De Luca, Araldo and Kent R. Weeks, eds. *Im Tal der Könige. Von Grabkunst und Totenkult der ägyptischen Herrscher.* Augsburg: Weltbild, 2001.

Description de l'Egypte ou Recueil des observations et des recherches qui ont été faites en Egypte pendant l'expédition de l'armée française publié sous les ordres de Napoléon Bonaparte. Vol. II, 1st ed. Paris: 1818.

Description de l'Egypte ou Recueil des observations et des recherches qui ont été faites en Egypte pendant l'expédition de l'armée française. Vol. III, 2nd ed. Paris: Charles Louis Fleury Panckoucke, 1821.

Diodorus Siculus. *Library of History I,* trans. C. H. Oldfather. Cambridge, MA: Loeb Classical Library, 1933.

Dodson, Aidan. *Amarna Sunset: Nefertiti, Tutankhamun, Ay, Horemheb and the Egyptian Counterrevolution.* Cairo: American University in Cairo Press, 2009.

___. *Poisoned Legacy: The Fall of the Nineteenth Egyptian Dynasty.* Cairo: American University in Cairo Press, 2010.

Donadoni Roveri, Anna Maria, ed. *Egyptian Civilization: Monumental Art.* Milan: Electra, 1989.

Drenkhahn, Rosemarie. *Die Elephantine-Stele des Sethnacht und ihr historischer Hintergrund.* Ägyptologische Abhandlung, no. 36. Wiesbaden: Harrassowitz, 1980.

___. "Ein Nachtrag zu Tausret." *Göttinger Miszellen* 43 (1981): 19–22.

Eaton-Krauss, Marianne. "Sety-Merenptah als Kronprinz Merenptahs." *Göttinger Miszellen* 50 (1981):15–21.

Fazzini, Richard A., James F. Romano, and Madeleine E. Cody. *Art for Eternity: Masterworks from Ancient Egypt.* New York: Brooklyn Museum of Art, Scala Publishers, 1999.

Franken, H. J. "The Excavations at Deir 'Allā in Jordan: 2nd Season." *Vetus Testamentum* 11:4 (1961): 361–372.

___. *Excavations at Deir 'Allā: The Late Bronze Age Sanctuary.* Louvain: Peters Press, 1992.

Friedman, Florence D. "The Menkaure Dyad(s)." In *Egypt and Beyond: Essays Presented to Leonard H. Lesko,* ed. Stephen E. Thompson and Peter Der Manuelian, 109–144. Providence, RI: Department of Egyptology, Brown University, 2008.

Frood, Elizabeth. *Biographical Texts from Ramessid Egypt.* Atlanta: Society of Biblical Literature, 2007.

Gaballa, G. A. "Some Nineteenth Dynasty Monuments in Cairo Museum." *Bulletin de l'Institut Français d'Archéologie Orientale* 71 (1972): 134.

Gardiner, Alan H. "The Tomb of Queen Twosre." *Journal of Egyptian Archaeology* 40 (1954): 40–44.

———. "Only One King Siptah and Twosre Not His Wife." *Journal of Egyptian Archaeology* 44 (1958): 12–22.

———. *Egypt of the Pharaohs.* Oxford: Clarendon Press, 1961.

Gillam, Robyn A. "Priestesses of Hathor: Their Function, Decline and Disappearance." *Journal of the American Research Centre in Egypt* 32 (1995): 211–237.

Goedicke, Hans. "Was Magic Used in the Harem Conspiracy against Ramesses III?" *Journal of Egyptian Archaeology* 49 (1963): 71–92.

Grandet, Pierre. *Le Papyrus Harris I (BM 9999).* 2 vols. Bibliothèque d'étude, no. 109:1–2, Cairo: Institut Français d'Archéologie Orientale du Caire, 1994.

———. "L'execution du chancelier Bay O. IFAO 1864." *Bulletin de Institut Français d'Archéologie Orientale du Caire* 100 (2000): 339–356.

Grajetzki, Wolfram. *Ancient Egyptian Queens: A Hieroglyphic Dictionary.* London: Golden House, 2005.

Green, Lyn. "Queen as Goddess: The Religious Role of Royal Women in the Late-Eighteenth Dynasty." *Amarna Letters I* (1992): 28–41.

Harris, J. R. and K. Weeks, "X-raying the Pharaohs." *Natural History* 81:7 (August/September, 1972): 61.

Hawass, Zahi and Sandro Vannini. *Bilder der Unsterblichkeit. Die Totenbücher aus den Königsgräbern in Theben.* Mainz: Philipp von Zabern, 2006.

Hay, Robert. *Egyptian Collection 1824–1838.* Vol. VIII. *Thebes. Tombs of the Kings.* Mss. in British Museum, London. MSS 25642.

Hayes, W. *Scepter of Egypt,* Vol. II, rev. ed. New York: Metropolitan Museum of Art, 1990.

Helck, Wolfgang. "Drei Ramessidische Daten." *Studien zur Altägyptischen Kultur* 17 (1990): 205–214.

———. "Die Datierung des Papyrus Greg." In *Gedenkschrift für Winfried Barta, Htp dj n Hzj,* ed. D. Kessler and R. Schulz, 199–213. Münchner Ägyptologische Untersuchungen, Frankfurt: Peter Lang 1995.

Herodotus. *The Histories II.* Trans. A. de Sélincourt, revised with introduction and notes by J. Marincola. London: Viking/Penguin, 1996.

Hölscher, U. *The Mortuary Temple of Ramesses III,* Part I, Vol. III of *The Excavation of Medinet Habu.* Chicago: University of Chicago Oriental Institute, 1941.

Hornung, Erik. *Das Amduat. Die Schrift des verborgenen Raumes.* Teil I: *Text;* Teil II: *Übersetzung und Kommentar.* Ägyptologische Abhandlungen, no. 7, Wiesbaden: Harassowitz, 1963.

Kitchen, Kenneth A. *Ramesside Inscriptions, Historical and Biographical.* Vol. IV, *Merenptah and the Late Nineteenth Dynasty.* Oxford: Blackwell, 1982.

———. "Tausret." In *Lexikon der Aegyptologie.* Vol. VI, cols. 244–245. Wiesbaden: Harrassowitz, 1986.

———. *Ramesside Inscriptions, Translated and Annotated, Translations.* Vol. IV, *Merenptah and the Late Nineteenth Dynasty.* Oxford: Blackwell, 2003.

Legrain, Georges. *Statue et Statuettes de Rois et de Particuliers.* Cairo: Institut Français d'Archéologie Orientale du Caire Press, 1906.

Lehner, Mark. *The Pyramid Tomb of Hetepheres and the Satellite Pyramid of Khufu.* Mainz: Verlag Philipp von Zabern, 1985.

Lepsius, Richard C. *Denkmäler aus Ägypten und Äthiopien: nach den Zeichnungen der von Seiner Majestät dem Könige von Preussen Friedrich Wilhelm IV. nach diesen Ländern gesendeten und in den Jahren 1842–1845 ausgeführten wissenschaftlichen Expedition.* Berlin: Nicolaische Buchhandlung, 1849–1859.

___. *Denkmäler aus Ägypten und Äthiopien.* Vol. 3. Leipzig: Eduard Naville, 1900.

Lesko, Barbara S. "Queen Kharmerernebty II and Her Sculpture." In *Ancient Egyptian and Mediterranean Studies in Memory of William A. Ward,* ed. Leonard H. Lesko, 149–162. Providence, RI: Brown University, 1998.

Lichtheim, Miriam. *Ancient Egyptian Literature.* Vol. I, *The Old and Middle Kingdoms.* Berkeley: University of California Press, 1974.

___. *Ancient Egyptian Literature.* Vol. II, *The New Kingdom.* Berkeley: University of California Press, 1976.

Lilyquist, Christine. "Treasures from Tell Basta: Religion, Politics, and Art in an International Age." *Journal of the Metropolitan Museum of Art* 46 (forthcoming).

Maderna-Sieben, Claudia. "Der historische Abschnitt des Papyrus Harris I."*Göttinger Miszellen* 123 (1991): 57–90.

Marciniak, Marek. *Les inscriptions hiératiques du temple de Thoutmosis III.* Warsaw: PWN-Editions scientifiques de Pologne, 1974.

Marée, Marcel. "A Jar from Sidon with the name of Pharaoh-Queen Tawosret." *Archaeology & History in the Lebanon* 24 (Winter 2006): 121–128.

Maspero, George. "King Siphtah and Queen Tauosrît." In *The Tomb of Siphtah: The Monkey Tomb and the Gold Tomb,* ed. Theodore M. Davis, xiii–xxix. London: A. Constable, 1908.

McCarthy, Heather Lee. "Rules of Decorum and Expressions of Gender Fluidity in Tawosret's Tomb." In *Sex and Gender in Ancient Egypt: "Don Your Wig for a Joyful Hour,"* ed. C. Graves-Brown, 83–113. Swansea: Classical Press of Wales, 2008.

Moran, William L. *The Amarna Letters.* Baltimore: Johns Hopkins University Press, 1992.

Naville, Édouard. *The Temple of Deir el-Bahari.* 7 vols. London: Egypt Exploration Fund, 1895–1908.

Nelson, Harold H. *Medinet Habu.* Vol. IV, *Festival Scenes of Ramses III.* Oriental Institute Publications, no. 51. Chicago: Oriental Institute Press, 1940.

O'Connor, David and David P. Silverman, eds. *Ancient Egyptian Kingship.* Leiden: Brill, 1995.

Petrie, W. M. Flinders. *Six Temples at Thebes.* London: Bernard Quaritch, 1897.

___. *Royal Tombs of the First Dynasty.* Vol. I. London: Egypt Exploration Society, 1900.

___. *Methods and Aims in Archaeology.* London: Macmillan, 1904.

Plutarch. *Isis and Osiris, Moralia V.* Trans. F. C. Babbitt. Cambridge, MA: Loeb Classical Library, 1936.

Pococke, Robert. *A Description of the East, and Some Other Countries.* Vol. 1. London: W. Boyer, 1743.

Porter, Bertha and Rosalind Moss. *Topographical Bibliography of Ancient Egyptian Hieroglyphic Texts, Reliefs, and Paintings.* Vol. 2, *The Theban Necropolis: Royal Tombs and Smaller Cemeteries.* Oxford: Clarendon Press, 1964.

Pusch, E. B. "Tausret und Sethos II in der Rameses-Stadt." *Ägypten und Levante* IX (1999): 109.

Ratié, Suzanne. *La Reine Hatchepsout: Sources et Problèmes.* Leiden: E.J. Brill, 1979.

Redford, Susan. *The Harem Conspiracy: The Murder of Ramesses III.* Dekalb: Northern Illinois University Press, 2002.

Reeves, Carl Nicholas. *Valley of the Kings: The Decline of a Royal Necropolis.* Studies in Egyptology. London: Kegan Paul International, 1990.

Reeves, Carl Nicholas and Geoffrey T. Martin. "ARTP's 4th Season of Work, 2002: Where We Dug and What We Found." http://www.nicholasreeves.com/item.aspx?category= Writing&id=101.

Reeves, Carl Nicholas and Richard H. Wilkinson. *The Complete Valley of the Kings.* London: Thames and Hudson, 1996.

Reisner, George A. and William Stevenson Smith. *A History of the Giza Necropolis II: The Tomb of Hetepheres the Mother of Cheops.* Cambridge, MA: Harvard University Press, 1955.

Robins, Gay. "A Critical Examination of the Theory that the Right to the Throne of Egypt Passed through the Female Line in the 18th Dynasty." *Göttinger Miszellen* 62 (1983): 67–77.

____. *Women in Ancient Egypt.* London: British Museum Press, 1993.

Roehrig, Catharine Hershey. "The Eighteenth Dynasty Titles Royal Nurse (*mn't nswt*), Royal Tutor (*mn'nswt*), and Foster Brother/Sister of the Lord of the Two Lands (*sn/snt mn'n nb t3wy*)." Ph.D. dissertation, 1990 (UMI Dissertation Services, 9103856).

____, ed. *Hatshepsut: From Queen to Pharaoh. Exhibition Catalogue.* New York: Metropolitan Museum of Art, 2005.

____. "Some Thoughts on Queens' Tombs in the Valley of the Kings." In *Thebes and Beyond: Studies in Honor of Kent R. Weeks,* eds. Z. Hawass and S. Ikram, 181–196. Supplément aux *Annales du Service des antiquités de l'Egypte,* no. 41. Cairo: Supreme Council of Antiquities, 2010.

____. "Two Royal Canopic Boxes from the Tomb of Siptah (KV 47), in the Metropolitan Museum of Art." (in progress).

Rosellini, Ippolito. *I monumenti dell' Egitto e della Nubia.* 3 vols. Pisa: N. Capurro, 1832–1844.

Roth, Ann Macy. "The Absent Spouse: Patterns and Taboos in Egyptian Tomb Decoration." *Journal of the American Research Center in Egypt* 36 (1999): 37–53.

____. "Models of Authority: Hatshepsut's Predecessors in Power." In *Hatshepsut: From Queen to Pharaoh,* ed. Catharine H. Roehrig et al., 9–14. New York: Metropolitan Museum of Art, 2005.

Roth, Silke. *Die Königsmutter des alten Ägypten von der Frühzeit biss zum Ende der 12. Dynastie.* Ägypten und Altes Testament, no. 46. Wiesbaden: Harrassowitz, 2001.

____. "Queen." In *UCLA Encyclopedia of Egyptology,* ed., Elizabeth Frood and Willeke Wendrich. http://repositories.cdlib.org/nelc/uee/1055. Los Angeles, CA: UCLA, 2009.

Scheel, Bernd. "The Power behind the Tomb." *Illustrated London News* 274:7057 (1986): 62–63.

Schulman, Alan R. "Ankhesenamun, Nofretity and the Amka Affair." *Journal of the American Research Centre in Egypt* 15 (1978): 43–48.

Shaw, Ian, ed. *The Oxford History of Ancient Egypt.* Oxford: Oxford University Press, 2000.

Simon-Boidot, Claire. "Canon et etalon dans la tombe de Taousret." *Chronique d'Égypte* 75:149 (2000): 30–46.

Singer, Itamar. "A Political History of Ugarit." In *Handbook of Ugaritic Studies,* eds. Wilfred Watson and Nicolas Wyatt , 713ff. Leiden: Brill, 1999.

Thomas, Elizabeth. *The Royal Necropoleis of Thebes.* Princeton: [privately published], 1966.

Troy, Lana. "Ahhotep—A Source Evaluation." *Göttinger Miszellen* 35 (1979): 81–91.

———. *Patterns of Queenship in Ancient Egyptian Myth and History.* Uppsala: Acta Universitatis Upsaliensis, 1986.

Tyldesley, Joyce A. *Daughters of Isis: Women of Ancient Egypt.* New York: Viking/Penguin, 1994.

———. *Hatchepsut: The Female Pharaoh.* London: Viking/Penguin, 1996.

———. *Nefertiti: Egypt's Sun Queen,* rev. ed. London: Viking/Penguin, 2005.

———. *Chronicle of the Queens of Egypt: From Early Dynastic Times to the Death of Cleopatra.* London: Thames and Hudson, 2006.

———. *Cleopatra: Egypt's Last Queen.* London: Profile Books, 2008.

———. *Myths and Legends of Ancient Egypt.* London: Viking/Penguin, 2010.

Verner, Miroslav. *The Pyramids: Their Archaeology and History.* Trans. Steven Rendall. London: Atlantic Books, 2002.

Waddell, W.G. *Manetho.* Cambridge, MA: Loeb Classical Library, 1940.

Weeks, Kent R. "Theban Mapping Project." http://www.thebanmapping project.com/. Cairo: 1998–2008.

———., ed. *Atlas of the Valley of the Kings.* Publications of the Theban Mapping Project, no. 1. Cairo: American University in Cairo Press, 2000.

———. *The Treasures of Luxor and the Valley of the Kings.* Vercelli: White Star, 2005; Cairo: American University in Cairo Press, 2005.

Wilkinson, Richard H. "The Tausert Temple Project: 2004 and 2005 Seasons." *The Ostracon: Journal of the Egyptian Study Society* 16:2 (Summer, 2005): 7–12.

———. "Excavation in the Time of V.S. Golenischev: W. M. F. Petrie's Work at the Tausert Memorial Temple." In *Ancient Egypt,* Vol. II, ed. V. V. Solkin, 160–165, Pl. 69–73. Moscow: Association of Ancient Egypt Studies, 2006.

———. "The Tausert Temple Project 2006 Season." *The Ostracon: Journal of the Egyptian Study Society* 17:2 (Fall, 2006): 9–12.

———. "The Tausert Temple Project 2007 Season." *The Ostracon: Journal of the Egyptian Study Society* 18:1 (Summer, 2007): 3–10.

———. "The Tausert Temple Project 2008 Season." *The Ostracon: Journal of the Egyptian Study Society* 19:1 (Winter, 2008): 3–7.

———. "The Tausert Temple Project 2009 Season." *The Ostracon: Journal of the Egyptian Study Society* 20:1 (Winter, 2009): 3–13.

———. "Six Seasons at Thebes: The University of Arizona Tausert Temple Project." In *Thebes and Beyond: Studies in Honor of Kent R. Weeks,* ed. Z. Hawass and S. Ikram, 17–177. Supplément aux *Annales du Service des antiquites de l'Egypte,* no. 41. Cairo: Supreme Council of Antiquities, 2010.

———. "The Tausert Temple Project 2009–10 Season." *The Ostracon: Journal of the Egyptian Study Society* 21:1 (Fall 2010): 3–11.

———. "The Memorial Temple of Tausert: Was It Ever Completed?" In *The Temples of Millions of Years: Science and New Technologies Applied to Archaeology,* ed. Christian Leblanc. Acts of the International Symposium, Luxor, January 2010. Cairo: Supreme Council of Antiquities, 2011.

———. "The Tausert Temple Project 2010–11 Season." *The Ostracon: Journal of the Egyptian Study Society* 22:1 (Fall 2011): forthcoming.

___. "Tausret." In *Blackwell Encyclopedia of Ancient History*, ed. R. Bagnall et al. Oxford: Wiley-Blackwell, forthcoming.

Wilkinson, Toby. *Early Dynastic Egypt*. London: Routledge, 1999.

Yoyotte, Jean. "Un Souvenir du 'Pharaon' Taousert en Jordanie." *Vetus Testamentum* 12:4 (October 1962): 464–469.

Yurco, Frank. J. "Amenmesse: Six Statues at Karnak." *Metropolitan Museum Journal* 14 (1979): 15–31.

Ziegler, Christiane, ed. *Queens of Egypt: From Hetepheres to Cleopatra*. Monaco: Somogy Editions d'Art, 2008.

Index